Back from Sanity's Edge

To Jennifer

A very anointed and
Powerful writer. Let
God Continue to bring
Out the wealth of wisdom
that is deep down in
Your Soul.

Love
Denese J. Smith
5/2004   313-862-4...

Back from Sanity's Edge

◆

Trusting God Through the Pain

Denise A. Smith

iUniverse, Inc.

New York Lincoln Shanghai

Back from Sanity's Edge
Trusting God Through the Pain

iUniverse, Inc.

For information address:
iUniverse, Inc.
2021 Pine Lake Road, Suite 100
Lincoln, NE 68512
www.iuniverse.com

Unless otherwise stated, all Scripture references come from the King James Version of the Bible.

Though this book is nonfiction, some of the names are fictitious.

Author's photograph © Photography by Thomason, Summerville, SC

ISBN: 0-595-30907-0

Printed in the United States of America

To the Lord, my God and Savior, Jesus Christ, and to all families that have lost their loved ones through acts of violence. And to those who have been victims of crime, and survived.

"And we know that all things
work together for good to them that love God,
to them who are the called according to his purpose."

—*(Romans 8:28)*

Contents

A special thank you goes out to family and friends who endured with me through all the different challenges I faced. To name a few, I recognize my parents, O'Dell and Barbara Nelson, my sister, Cheryl Foster, and my brothers O'Dell B. (Butch), Darrell K., and Rex K. Nelson. I could not have written this book without the love of my children, Aaron, Angela, and Adam Thomason, and my grandson Nathan. Where would I be without my partners, Saun and Charalyn (Chally) Nelson? We call ourselves, "The Three Musketeers." To my husband, L. C. Smith, Jr., who, seven years ago, married me with all the emotional damage, I love you. I thank you for all your help.

Special thanks go out to all my mentors who groomed me to be the person I am today. The list includes the late Bishop David Ellis, and his wife, Wilma, Bishop Charles Ellis III, and his wife, Crissette, Pastors Norman and Barbara Chaney, and the late Pastor Lottie Glenn Richey Gibson. My current pastor, Stanley E. Rayford and his lovely wife Robin, and my church family Restoration Fellowship Tabernacle, have been kind. My sincere appreciation goes out to my prayer partners Sandra King, Anita Norwood, Delorese Goodson, Sonja Bell-Johnson, Leitha Anderson, Jerry Jones-Davis, Edna Johnson, Ronnie Hastie, Grace Stewart, Toni Hunter, Venus Thues, Linda Fegins, and Minetta Hare. I thank The Lydia Prayer Circle, and The Lydia Circle Christian Businesswomen.

Minister Mary Edwards, Wanda Burnside, and The Called and Ready Writers Guild, helped me to believe I could write. I thank Pamela Perry, and the American Christian Writers Association, Detroit Chapter, because they convinced me that excuses were not acceptable. The Detroit Writers Guild, then headed by Sharon Stanford, is where I began to learn the craft of writing. My critique group, Linda Fegins, Rain Africa Reign, Angela Thomason, Aaron Thomason, and Adam Thomason, helped with useful comments, and even with critiquing, correcting and rebuking, when I kept shuffling my feet. To Fran and Don Pratt who labored as my editors and as my midwives to help give birth to the finished product, I say thanks. To my quality control team, L. C., Angela Thomason, Sharon Stanford, Rhea Norwood, Richard

Williams (The Creative Creature), and Ron Kenner (RKedit), thanks for the untiring efforts. Without your final touches, I would not have the finished masterpiece of love.

Warm loving appreciation goes out to my former church family, Greater Grace Temple, in Detroit, Michigan, including the Hon. Bishop Charles Ellis III and the late Bishop David L. Ellis. This church family loved me through the pain. They wrapped their loving arms around me and helped me through the storm. I thank the Children's Ministry staff, and the children, for their outpouring of unconditional love. I want to express my gratitude, to the brave and dedicated men and women who work for the Michigan Department of Corrections. Credit and appreciation goes to the Detroit Police Department, especially Officer (Victor) Darnell Williams, who prayed for me at the crime scene. The Detroit Emergency Medical Services technicians were efficient and quick. Not only did they try to ease the pain, they also tried to get me help as quickly as possible. The medical team at Grace Hospital, who weren't actors as on the series *ER* but people, dedicated to saving real lives. They also deserve an expression of my gratitude. I will never forget the chaplains and medical staff who labored and fought for me to live, and not die. They comforted me any time of the day or night, when I just couldn't make sense of what was going on.

Congratulations to my book, prayer, accountability partner, Pamela Osborne, who finished her first book, *Bread and Butter*. God heard our prayers. To the Midwives for Jesus, Nancy Smith, Vivian Williams, Ann Weaver, Ivy Caddell, and Anita Norwood; thanks for letting me lead the group. Your love and prayers helped me to complete my manuscript. To La Dean Birkhead-Perez, our friendship began on-the-job but transformed into a love that helped us to weather the storms of life. I say, thanks, for not leaving me alone in my misery.

To all the people who held a prayer vigil in the hospital waiting room while the surgeons did their best to save me, I say thanks. To Kathy, Debbie, and Ann, who worked with my mom to get me help and make me comfortable, I will always remember your labor of love.

Since there is no way to remember everyone, I send out a general thank you, to make sure, that I recognize everyone who had a hand in my recovery. The list is too long to write. I may have forgotten your name, but God hasn't. Please charge it to my head, and not my heart.

Foreword

Back from Sanity's Edge helped me to deal with my "issues." It pulled me off the edge of mental illness and brought me back to soundness of mind. Too many people today bury their pain to avoid dealing with it. I learned that hiding mine did not resolve the problem.

When Denise Smith revealed her scars, it made me want to show mine, too. It seemed correct to touch them. I no longer felt alone. Reading her story gave me permission to say, "Ouch, that hurts." Healing for me is faster when I seek support to confront my issues. This book did that for me. Her triumph gave me inspiration to make a comeback. It boosted my self-esteem, and my confidence in God.

Too many times I let others decide my fate by accepting his or her assessment of me. I gave them the power to control how long I hurt and when to get over it. As I now understand it, that was insanity. *Back from Sanity's Edge,* empowered me to be responsible for my own life.

Being on the edge made me want to know, "Is there anyone out there who cares?" The answer is yes. And now life begins.

Sandra King, of Inner Dominion Ministries

Introduction

How can a mind endure so much at one time? I faced violence, bribery, divorce, lies, depression, anger, and thoughts of suicide. My prayer for you, dear reader, is that this book will help you find the answer. Like Job, in the Bible, I experienced a series of setbacks. I almost went crazy. The question *"Why?"* echoed constantly in my mind. The racing accusations screamed at me, as if these setbacks were my fault. Rehashing, rehearsing, and reliving events over and again made me wonder if insanity was my expected end. Why wouldn't the chatter stop? Was I superhuman, able to bear the impossible? *No.* If not, then what was it that kept my mind and spirit intact?

After being shot, help for recovery in the literature was archaic at best. Finding books written by gunshot victims was impossible. I read books written by families of the deceased, stories of loss, but no one wrote about the struggles of the *injured* toward recovery. So I read other stories by victims of life's afflictions. I felt like a dinosaur trapped in the millennium—no new niche to fit into. People were sympathetic but didn't know what to do. Efforts to set up a new life were slow and awkward. I badly needed some camaraderie. I needed to hear someone else's tale of woe and the steps *he or she* took to recovery. I wanted to ask specific and private questions. Did their life change? What were the reactions of family and friends? I wanted to hear about the emotional side of recovery.

I read books about such crises as cancer, bombings, molestation and other types of devastation, but no one captured on paper the likes of my struggle to survive a brutal shooting. Approaches such as self-help books, anonymous 12-step programs, a mental health hospital program, and other group meetings helped some. They were emotional bandages but they did not resolve the problem. Divine intervention was needed—a miracle. Now I am compelled to share the miracle with you.

During that season, I failed to keep pace with everyone else. I lived an alternate existence. *Girl Interrupted,* written by Susanna Kaysen, was a valued read. She recorded life in a mental institution and all of the related drama associated with confinement. She clearly depicted her mental illness. I identified with her assessment.

I wasn't insane but I didn't feel normal either. I guess I slipped into one of the alternate worlds described by Susanna. My *today* was so strange that I could not fathom what to do. I was a foreigner in my own life.

"God, where are You?" I asked. "How could You let so many hurtful events happen to me, at once? After all, I'm Your child."

When no immediate response came, I felt edgy; as though walking on a tightrope. Barely functioning, I felt one careless step would drop me into an abyss of destruction. Trying to define the word "edge," I looked it up in *The New International Webster's Pocket Dictionary:* "A border or margin; the cutting part of a blade; a dividing line. To create a border; to sharpen; to advance gradually." That definition helped me focus on the emotions I was experiencing. I felt as though I were walking on the "borderline" of a nervous breakdown. My hope in God kept me from crossing that border. I had to trust Him, or accept the fate of going mad. Fear tormented my soul so much that I felt myself gradually heading toward the brink of suicide.

Knowing that an untimely death was not the answer, I decided to lock onto the only hope left; trusting God through the pain. Through this ordeal, I learned that hard times are opportunities to grow. Strong faith comes after enduring the fiery trials of life. Events such as spousal infidelity, estrangement and divorce forced me to examine how much of my trust was in God and how much of it was in me. I needed to know whether I was a "fair-weather Christian" or a warrior in God's Army. Was I going to make the transition to midlife smoothly, or give up as I sought to rebuild my life?

People go to the edge of rationality for many different reasons. Guilt and shame drove me there. Somewhere, inside, I felt that I had caused the problems and the violence; that I deserved it for being an imperfect human being. The "ifs" tormented me. Perhaps, I thought, I could have avoided the pain "if" I selected better choices that day…"if" I had never gone back to the job…"if" I had selected another career.

My primary purpose for writing this book is to keep people "on the edge" from falling off. I am sharing my story to let them know there will be brighter days coming—if they come to God, fully trust Him and obey Him no matter what.

I learned that:

- What I do (vocation) is not who I am

- I can reinvent myself at any time

- Leaning on God is important to overcoming troubles

- Recovery is hard work

- Restoration is worth the effort

Today the overriding theme in my life is Romans 8:28: *"And we know that all things work together for the good to them that love God, to them who are the called according to His purpose."*

1

The Eve of Death

My life, as a "Good Samaritan," almost ended on the cold, hard pavement in Detroit, Michigan, on December 8, 1992. When I recall the events of that day I still fight the influence of the small voices inside my head. They accuse me of recklessness. They whisper constantly: *It's your fault. It has to be. Good, God-fearing folks don't have all this misfortune happen to them all at once. You weren't careful enough. Everyone told you the job was dangerous, but did you listen? Now look at you—a has-been. Disabled. What do you have to show for it but scars and painful memories? You need to start thinking more about yourself.*

Somehow I believe the events of that hellish evening were preventable. I followed the safety protocol. Being cautious worked—until that day. How could this happen to me? In truth I wanted to cheer up an unhappy sister-in-law by buying her a birthday cake. Wasn't that a noble task? Being a self-sacrificing Christian?

I woke early, about four o'clock in the morning, disturbed in my spirit and agonized about my impending divorce. *Single again.* Did I waste seventeen years of my life? My prayer that morning centered on the new life ahead of me. The thought of it hurt.

"Good morning, Lord. Me again. I know it is earlier than usual, but I just can't sleep. I hate divorce as a conflict resolution. I exhausted the other choices: counseling, prayer, and patience; they all failed. When I said, 'I do,' I meant it to be, 'until death do us part.'"

After a pause, I heard a quiet reply from God.

"Denise, you only had one of the two votes to keep this marriage going."

"Well, yes, Lord, that's true."

"He is gone! Pick up the pieces and trust me through the pain."

"But, God, why does it hurt so much?"

"Dear one, you need to let it go."

"God, I am trying."

"Denise, it is hard to do when you are lonely?"

"Uh-huh."

"Left for another woman doesn't feel so good, does it?"

"No, Lord, it doesn't."

"I am with you. I will never leave you."

God knew how to unmask the truth.

"God, is it because I am no longer 140 pounds? I am not beautiful enough? If I were a little nicer, would he still be here?"

"Listen my child; he wanted to go. There is nothing you can do."

Just at that moment I remembered a snippet of conversation, between Mortimer and the judge during the final divorce hearing.

Judge Thomas asked, "Mr. Thomason do you want this divorce?"

He said intensely, "Yes!"

My legs began to shake, and my sweaty palms grew cold as I heard his answer. He didn't want to spend another moment married to me.

Judge Thomas continued, *"I have examined the facts and agree the marriage union has decayed beyond repair. Because of 'irreconcilable differences', I will grant this divorce."*

Those words left me upset. For the first time, my doctor prescribed high blood pressure medication to prevent a possible stroke.

I resumed my prayer: "God, I am not handling this well at all."

He said, with assurance, "If you just trust Me you will successfully come through this."

Reluctantly, I said, "I know, You're, right."

My unknown status was stressing me out. After two weeks, there was still no proof that my marital status had changed. Mortimer's attorney wanted the language changed in the divorce petition to make it more favorable for him.

It still echoed in my mind, the judge's final words at the last divorce hearing. "Your divorce is not official until the court-stamped documents are in your hand." To make sure I understood what he was saying, he requested an answer from me. I was so embarrassed when I answered him through chattering teeth. "Yes, Your Honor."

"Then, Denise," God said, interrupting my daydream, *"any day you will be free."*

"Yes," I answered, regretfully.

"This is not the end, but the beginning of a new chapter in your life," He added warmly.

"Well, yes, Lord." My voice cracked like an egg.

"My child, you should rejoice and not be sad. He no longer believes in the union with you. He is the unbeliever, and chose to leave. Let him. He stopped depending on Me for help. Instead, he became his own god."

I was at least halfway through my prayer when I addressed my next concern.

"God, something else is puzzling me. I don't understand the games people play. A man at work says he is my friend. He feels that he needs to shield me from men who could take advantage of a 'naïve church girl' like me. I just want to know who is going to shield me from him? He's a married man."

"I will." He said, with the voice of a proud father.

"Thanks." I said, relieved.

I hated to ask so many questions but I felt like David in Psalms 42. My soul felt cast down. I needed comforting and wisdom from my heavenly Father.

"Also, God, I am working scared everyday in a dangerous job as a probation tethering agent. Until recently, I saw it as a criminal justice, social worker job. But now I am afraid. These are some mean folks, people who would slap their own mother if she got out of line. Now that's mean. You know, families adore their mothers. I don't think my superiors see the whole picture."

"Hmm, but I know. You are never alone. Remember, I will always be by your side," God said, reassuring me.

"God, that is true. Still I feel the unfairness of my transfer."

"Why?"

"In April, Governor Mark Lane imposed cost saving measures."

"Yes."

"Well, he decided that confining criminals at home would be a big savings to the taxpayers of the State of Michigan."

"And?"

"Lord, it changed my life. That same month my superiors ordered me to work in that unit. This was the first time something like this had happened to me."

"I still don't see the problem."

"Since 1974, I have worked intermittently for the Department of Corrections; and I volunteered to work at new assignments. However, when it came to this assignment, I felt they treated me unfairly. I petitioned to stay at my original location, which was only six miles from my home. New employees received their preferences. I wanted mine, too."

"You wanted respect from your superiors?"

"Yes. Instead, the assistant administrator, Mr. Booth, said, 'I am not starting the new unit with rookies. I need your expertise. Petition denied.'"

"Why didn't you appeal the decision?"

"I didn't have enough strength to fight that decision, so I decided to conform. My new commute increased from six miles to thirteen. With rush hour traffic, my six-minute journey increased by some thirty minutes. On top of that, the clients scared me."

"Why?"

"Only high risk, dangerous criminals qualified for the program. At first, two co-workers, Malcolm and Daniel, who both carried guns, would escort me to dangerous house calls. After a while, they refused to go."

Malcolm said, 'It isn't worth risking my life any more, escorting you on house calls. Buy a gun, qualify, and carry it.'

Daniel agreed. 'Buy your own gun and learn how to use it. You are going to need it.' He laughed at the predicament that I was in."

"Denise, that doesn't seem fair."

"God, it wasn't, but I did just what they suggested."

"What's that?"

"I began carrying a gun. At first it gave me a sense of security, but after a while I learned to hate it. I didn't like the way it felt. After yesterday, I stopped carrying it. The way I see it, if attacked, I wouldn't get to it in time. My hands stay filled with my toolbox and the surveying equipment in tote. I will have to trust you for protection. If I can't…then I am as good as dead."

"I will protect you."

With these fears inside, I had to start my day with prayer. It helped to soothe the pain and rejection that I felt in my heart.

"Denise, I am always here," God whispered compassionately.

"God, I feel like nothing is going my way. Sometimes I feel like a fool. I must have *victim* written on my forehead."

"No. In fact a brighter tomorrow is coming. Just hold on a little longer. Love is coming your way, more than you imagine."

How exciting—love was coming my way. Imagine a Prince Charming who would sweep me off my feet. This revelation ended the prayer session.

"God, thanks for listening."

2

Set-Up

Equipped with a clear word from the Lord, I started my day energized by my warm thoughts.

I can't wait to see what God has in-store for me. I'm going to dress as if, 'Mr. Right', will find me today. Who can resist a, 'lady-in-waiting', dressed up in her finest? Amused, I continued with my morning rituals.

About 5:30 that morning I drank coffee in the breakfast nook with Saun, my sister-in-law. She replaced Mortimer. I am not sure whether my brother, Darrell, put her out or she left. But on August 24th Saun called about midnight.

"Nisey, Darrell kicked me out. I have nowhere to go. Can I come over to your house to spend the night?" she asked, weakly.

"Sure." I said, agreeing, but puzzled.

I took her in, since her family lived-in Thailand. This overnight visit eventually lasted almost two years.

Saun and I first met at Detroit's Metro Airport. Darrell was on active duty in the Air Force. He met Saun in Germany. They married, and soon Saun became pregnant. Darrell wanted her to have the best medical care, so he sent her to the United States to live, with my parents, until he got permission for a leave of absence.

Saun looked like an angel of mercy. Long flowing jet-black hair flowed about her face. Her big, brown, slanted eyes set within a flawless olive-brown, heart shaped face. She wore a black and white, size zero pantsuit. She seemed a frail, petite woman. Not so! She did not need my protection. Once she opened her mouth, her speech shattered the angelic persona. Saun's words were as spicy as her food. She could make a sailor blush no matter which language she spoke. I called her trilingual—fluent in Thai, English, and profanity. When angered, her heavy accent did not obscure the fiery words she used to tell an opponent off.

This woman, only 5'2", didn't need my help if in trouble. As a small child, she had learned self-defense. If she didn't hit a man in his groin, then she would throw him over her back in one easy swoop. Once on his back, she would mount his chest or neck with a foot of triumph. She knew how to stay safe.

It was Saun's 41st birthday. In our house, birthdays were special, so I planned a celebration dinner. Usually I would bake the cake, but I was on a diet. Having lost ten pounds, I didn't want to sabotage my progress. So I asked Donetta Green, a woman at our church, to bake a pound cake. That was the only cake Saun ate.

"Happy Birthday, Saun." I said, with enthusiasm.

"Thank you." She said, smiling.

"Remember, after work, we are having a dinner celebration. Donetta from church baked you a cake. The pick up time is 5:30. What time do you get off work today?" I asked Saun.

"6 p.m." She replied.

"I get off at 5:00. I will pick it up and meet you at the house," I said, with authority.

"That sounds great," she said.

We finished our usual morning chitchat and then dressed for work.

My daily routine after work was to go home and spend time with my children: Adam, 12, Angela, 13, and Aaron, 15. My concern centered on them, since my husband, Mortimer (Mort) Thomason's, departure nine months prior. Regrouping my life as a single parent took some doing, and not just for me. Aaron, the oldest son, took the helm as the man of our house. His 6' 8" stature made him look like he could handle the job, with shoulders broad enough to carry the world. But he, too, was just a kid trying to protect his mom and family.

"I am the head of the house now," he would say, flashing that charming, playful smile. He waited to see what reaction he would get from me.

"I am still in charge, and don't you forget it," I would snap back at him. He would laugh, once he realized that I was playing with him. Goofing around like that was good for a few chuckles. Sometimes he would chastise his brother and sister, or at least he'd try. Other times he'd try to tell me what to do. I would remind him who was in charge. At those times, he remembered that he was just a child, having to walk in some big vacant shoes left by his father.

Adam, on the other hand, wasn't trying to grow up faster than he should. He was a typical African-American adolescent. His wardrobe consisted of baggy pants mounted low on his hips, as if they were getting ready to fall off. He wore big, oversized shirts, like the hip-hop singers. He disliked wearing no-name gym shoes, because it messed up his 'style.' He was still discovering himself, when the separation occurred.

Adam did not like being home alone. He wanted to feel safe the way he used to when Mort lived with us. His dad worked the midnight shift while I worked the day shift. This arrangement offered twenty-four hour coverage for the children. We both loved them and wanted them to feel secure.

The house routine changed, and sometimes Adam was left home alone. This new arrangement left him feeling vulnerable. Sometimes he endured at least an hour by himself until Angie came home. I'd talk to him by telephone, from work, to calm his uneasiness. Other times, Saun's work schedule was flexible enough to keep him company. (On any other day I would have called Adam just before I left work to let him know I would arrive home soon. However, that day, my clients kept me so busy that I forgot to call and tell him I wasn't coming straight home.)

Angie was the other mother of the house. She protected Adam. I could trust her to come straight home from school, and comfort him, until an adult arrived home. Angie's maturity surpassed her natural years. She had displayed that trait since birth, earning the nickname, "old lady." Her Grandma Rose looked at her in the hospital, when she was only hours old, and commented, "that girl has an old spirit, she has been here before." That old spirited girl helped to make life easier for me, when Aaron was absent.

At thirteen, a beautiful young woman was replacing the little girl. God blessed Angie with a perfect set of white teeth, to accent her beauty. She transformed like a caterpillar into a butterfly. Her most glaring flaws, like most teenagers, were her pimples. Oily skin was the culprit. Angela's new softness and curves didn't go unnoticed by the young men in the neighborhood.

She didn't have time to play the games that boys wanted her to play. She planned to be a doctor. She was only thirteen, attending Cass Technical High School majoring in Chem-Bio, and smart. Her brother called her a "nerd." She was a chip off the old block. I too heard a similar nickname at thirteen.

Being a single mom was hard, and sticking to a routine was a must. To survive, I had to juggle all the responsibilities successfully. Breaking protocol sometimes resulted in costly outcomes, like forgetting to pick up a child at a sports practice or which child's attitude landed them in detention that day.

That night, I was not thinking straight. I had a second errand to run after leaving Donetta's. My father, O'Dell, was finally retiring at 66, after more than 30 years of service as a federal civil servant, and I needed to give him the money for my ticket to his retirement dinner. The deadline was soon approaching and I didn't want to miss it.

After I pick the cake up from Donetta's, I will go to Dad's. This makes for a long day when everything hurts. My knees are throbbing. How could I have left the Motrin at home on my dresser?

I promised myself that once I finished these errands I could go home, kick my boots off, and slip into my pajamas. I struggled daily with my painful knee. Though I returned to work, my left knee had not fully recovered. My kneecap hurt and it wobbled. I longed for the day when everything stopped hurting. My knee and my heart both were throbbing, as though they were competing for my attention. As I drove down the expressway, I realized I forgot to call Adam.

As soon as I get to Donetta's, I'll call him. Traffic's light this evening, and I'm making good time. I told her 5:30, but it looks like I am going to get there early.

As I approached the well-kept homes and manicured lawns of her neighborhood, I noticed that her home was dark. She usually turned on her lights when she was expecting a guest. That night, everyone else's porch light was lit up except hers. I pulled into her drive and sat there a moment. I wasn't sure what to do. It was obvious that no one was home. Crime was out of control. The local media reported robberies and shootings, so I didn't want to get out. Neither did I want to sit in the car and wait. In 1992, a new crime began in Detroit—car jacking; thugs robbed motorists, at gunpoint, of their cars.

Finally, I got out of my car and stepped up on her porch where I rang the bell and then knocked. When no one answered, I quickly retreated to the car. Uneasy, I decided to go to my parents' home, only three blocks away. The nooks and crannies of their neighborhood were my familiar old childhood stomping grounds. Why was I afraid to wait that day? I shook off the uneasiness and headed toward my parents' home. They didn't know that I was coming.

3

Nightmare on Sorrento

As I drove along Sorrento Street toward my parents' home, I was looking forward to completing all my chores and going home. My mood reflected the dismal "report day" I had just completed. I had never experienced such a hassle from a client.

"Mr. Malone," I said, "I am not replacing the failing house surveillance equipment. My supervisor, Grace Jackson, felt three disabled units from your home were not just coincidental. Besides, your case originated outside Aspen County, so your fate is out of our hands."

"So what does that mean?"

"It means that I will ask the court to issue a warrant for violation of probation. You will have to go back before the sentencing judge to decide what your punishment will be. The sentencing judge sentenced you under the Habitual Offenders Act. This violation could send you to prison."

"I am not going to prison, Mrs. Thomason."

"Tell that to the judge, Mr. Malone. You failed to keep the probation agreement. You piled up too many curfew violations. I closed your courtesy probation supervision in this county. Your sentencing judge, in Denver County, will handle your case next."

I tried to be as professional as I could be. There is no way to explain to a person that his freedom is in jeopardy. But Mr. Malone was furious with me.

"Let me get this right—you closed my probation? Why? I can't go to prison. I need you to rethink that."

He pleaded with me twice that day to reverse my decision. He came back to see me a second time to persuade me not to seek a warrant for his arrest.

"I am going to give you one more chance to change your mind," he said.

"Mr. Malone, I have said all that I am going to say. You will have the opportunity to plead for mercy with the judge. It is out of my hands now. Wait to receive a notice, from the Denver County Clerk's office. Then you can set a date for your arraignment on the warrant."

Never before had I thrown a client out of my office, but this day was the exception. This man was insistent, and I wasn't going to budge. He was so determined to see me a second time that he slipped by the receptionist and came straight to my office. It shocked me when I saw this big, burly figure standing over me calling my name.

I thought he was gone. I walked him out personally. What does he want now? Trying to bribe me last month didn't work. What's his new angle this time? I better be cautious how I handle this man. It was his wife, who told me last month that he was violating his curfew. She said, "If he knew I called you, he would have me killed." This man didn't mind pushing people around.

"Mrs. Thomason, can't you give me one more chance? Another unit won't have the same problem. I promise you that."

"Mr. Malone, we have already discussed this matter. I have nothing left to discuss with you."

I walked him out of the office a second time. This time I told both the receptionist and my supervisor of this man's determination.

"Grace, I have a funny feeling, that this case is not going to go away easily."

She said, "Update his file, including the wife's call from last month, then recommend that a warrant be issued for violation of probation."

As I drove down the street, I kept reliving that scene. About a half block from Dad's house, I passed a man, who was wearing army fatigues. I paid him little heed, except to notice, even in the twilight, that a hood covered his head. It surprised me that I did not recognize his silhouette as that of anyone I grew up with in the neighborhood.

About 5:25, I arrived at Dad's house. I planned to be there only a few minutes. I would park in the driveway and stay just long enough to pay for Dad's retirement ticket, and to call the baker.

I was still uneasy, and concerned with a possible car jacking. The driveway left me vulnerable, so I decided to back out and park on the street. Before I stepped out of the car, I checked my surroundings. Right in front of me, I saw that same man walking past Dad's house. I waited for him to pass, and to walk further down the street. I watched him for a while, until it seemed safe to exit my car. Once safe, I grabbed my badge, number 423, and I carried it for identification. Then I decided not to carry my purse.

Mom is going to have a fit, I thought.

Mom's advice repeated in my head, *Denise, you need to stop leaving that purse in the car. One day someone is going to break in your car and steal it.*

Mom had cautioned me over and again not to leave it unprotected. Of course, I ignored her wisdom.

As if arguing with Mom, I thought, *it is too heavy to carry after a long, tiring, report day.* I took the money out of my wallet and wrote Donetta's phone number on a piece of paper. Then I put them both in my hand, rolled up them into a small cylinder, not visible to anyone, even me. One final time I looked to see if it was safe for me to exit my car. Then I exited the car and slowly walked up the driveway, favoring my left knee. It throbbed each agonizing step I took.

I can't wait until I get home. I am so tired. How could I leave my pain pills at home?

An inner voice cheered me on, *Come on, Denise, just a few more steps and you'll be inside.*

Then I heard a noise behind me like a dry leaf underfoot. I thought, *Impossible! How could there be dry, crisp leaves on the ground in early December?*

I glanced behind me to disprove my suspicions, but instead I saw someone rapidly approaching. It was blurry at first. The silhouette drew nearer. I determined that it was the hooded man—the same man whom I had seen walking down the street. Seconds later, the man was next to me, mumbling. I didn't know if he was friend or foe, but I realized I needed to make a quick decision. Do I run or not?

At the end of my medical leave of absence, Dr. Bledsoe said, "Any sudden moves will result in a fall." Since I couldn't run, I decided to turn and confront the man.

When he reached into his Desert Storm jacket and pulled out a black gun, I realized this was not a social visit. I also ruled out his being family or a friend. My mind reeled with questions. *What did he want? My purse—it was in the car.* All I was wearing were tiny gold earrings and a cheap Timex watch. I was sure he didn't want my black felt hat strapped under my chin, or my plus-size three-quarter-length tweed car coat. The most expensive apparel I was wearing that night were my size 11 black leather boots. Otherwise, a robber was wasting his time.

He was muttering something like, "Give it to me."

I hate people who mumble, but I was too scared to ask him to repeat it. I just looked at him without saying a word.

Then he said, clearly, "Scream and I'll shoot."

Terrified, and still securely gripping the money and address in my fists, I backed away from my assailant. I believed his intent was to use the gun. Somehow, he knew me. My knees hurt so much that I had to shift my weight periodically from one leg to the other. Shifting his position away from me, he acted like a man afraid of a Bruce Lee kick to his face. After all, at a height of 5'8" and weight of 250 pounds, I was not exactly a weakling. However, I do walk bent over because of congenital scoliosis of the spine.

I thought, *he has the gun, so why is he afraid of me? Does he know me? Does he know what I do for a living? Could he be a client I don't remember from years ago?*

Recalling self-defense lessons that taught us to make noise in times like these, I went into action. Bringing attention to the scene increases the chance for survival. Ignoring his warnings, I screamed at the top of my lungs, "Mama, Daddy!"

He smirked at my futile efforts to call for help and enjoyed watching me squirm.

I thought, *he's enjoying my fear.* His evil joy gave me moments in which I remembered another training. In Bible class, the late Pastor Lottie Glenn Richey Gibson taught us, "If you're ever in trouble, and don't know what to do, call out the name of Jesus. Supernatural help will arrive. God will send angels to your rescue."

The man still held a gun aimed at my chest. In desperate obedience to Pastor Gibson, I hollered one last time, "Jesus."

4

The Cloak of Darkness

The name "Jesus" agitated my assailant. His facial features contorted, his eyes bulged and mouth twisted. The corners of his mouth looked like the letter "Z". I thought he was having a stroke or seizure. The furrows on his forehead rippled into tight wavy lines. His sneer changed to rage. Then I saw something, seen only in science fiction movies. His face twisted into a grimace, and a neon-green ghoulish image appeared, as if his head had split in half. A hideous image oozed out. It resembled Casper the Friendly Ghost, but it was green, and not friendly. This presence was more threatening than the gun at my chest. The evil emanating from that man stung my nostrils. I could smell death in the air. I realized that it came to kill me. It embodied a presence of evil I had never met.

Petrified, I thought I was hallucinating, and was unable to believe what I saw. I had only seen such images in horror films or nightmares, but now I was wide-awake and fully conscious. My mind had seen into another dimension—that of raw evil—and it couldn't understand it.

"What in the world is this?" I thought.

I read stories in books about people delivered from demons that were greenish in color. Once, I saw such an image in the movie *The Exorcist*. Another time, in 1968, at age 15, I saw this same spirit when I was gravely ill with a fever. At 103 degrees, I became delirious and saw green witches on my bedposts, with visions of my friend Norman. Now, I realized the green I saw then was similar to the hue I saw that night.

Wide-eyed, I backed away from him. The heel on my boot got caught on a crack in the sidewalk.

Oh no, I hope I don't fall.

I lost my balance, and fell backward. It felt as though something or someone pulled me to the ground—as though a presence was with me. (I'd like to believe that God had dispensed angelic help.) My enemy stood over me, pointing the gun at my stomach.

This man is not playing. He is going to shoot me.

At that moment I had a close look at the menacing face. The green was gone and I saw his broad nostrils, throbbing with fury. His breathing quickened, heaving his chest up and down as if he were struggling to gasp air. Vapor escaped from his nose like a smokestack in winter. The Z mouth turned into an upside down U just like the shape of his mustache. I knew that I would never forget those features.

If I survive this mess, the police will get his description. I thought.

There was no doubt in my mind that he was going to shoot me. As he squeezed the trigger, I clenched my eyes shut, as tightly as my fists. I braced for the impact of the bullets. Nothing happened.

I opened my eyes. The gun misfired. I relaxed my stomach muscles and began breathing a sigh of relief.

It worked! The name of Jesus saved me!

He recocked that gun and cleared the jammed bullet. Once more he squeezed the trigger.

POW, POW, POW, POW, POW, went the sound of the assailant's 9-millimeter, semi-automatic pistol. Each bullet pierced my coat and flesh. Those small metal missiles of destruction seared through my body. The stinging force, at first, overwhelmed my senses so I felt nothing. But moments later, the pain registered. It caused me to curl up into a semi-fetal position.

Engulfed in pain, I wondered, "Why?"

The assailant handled the gun like a sharpshooter. The gun's recoil didn't bother him. He handled the gun as if he was comfortable with it; yet he seemed nervous. His nervousness resembled a drug addict in withdrawal.

I wonder why he shot me? If he needed a fix, why didn't he rob me? I tried to think through the pain. It was hard to do as I watched my bright red blood spill to the ground. I asked myself, *what did I do to this stranger?*

Fear kept me quiet, and he left without taking anything except, possibly, my life. He looked around to see if anyone heard the shots before he dashed off. Obviously, no one did. He left the scene unnoticed by anyone except me. He ran south on Sorrento, heading toward Outer Drive.

I felt vulnerable, lying on the cold, hard ground, and in agony. I could not move my right leg. It locked into a 90-degree right triangle. There was nothing to do but pray.

"Lord, please help me," I cried aloud.

5

Angels on Assignment

Now, an eerie silence followed. It served as a calming effect. Briefly, the pain numbed. I needed a plan. Thoughts crowded my mind. *Should I call for help? Am I going to live or die? If I die, the badge in my pocket will identify me. I wonder how will my family react to this? Who will take care of my children?*

I wasn't afraid to die. I had secured my everlasting life, in 1976, when I became a born-again Christian. I turned my face toward Heaven and said, "God, will I live?"

He answered: *I rerouted the bullets.*

I interpreted that meant life. Then I rehearsed in my heart, the morning prayer. I recalled the soothing words that God spoke.

Love is coming your way, more than you can imagine.

I have a future! I thought. Then I screamed for help.

"Help. Somebody, help me!"

At first, the noise from the bullets, and my cry, went unnoticed. Then, I heard a creaky door opening.

Thank God, it's Mr. Jackson, my parents' next door neighbor. He will rescue me!

It felt good to see a familiar face. He stuck his head out the door, and looked at me. He asked, "Who are you?"

Is he kidding? I thought.

Then, I answered him, and said, "Denise Thomason."

He replied, "I don't know you."

"I'm the Nelsons' daughter. Please tell my parents I am shot."

He repeated, "I don't know you." And he closed the door.

What was I going to do?
I began screaming again. "Help, somebody, help me."
In a few seconds a neighbor, Kathy, came to my aid.
"Denise, what happened?"
"I was going to see Mama and Daddy, and somebody shot me."
"What'd he do that for? Did you know him?
"No."
Kathy shivered and looked around to see if he was still there.
"Is he gone?"
"Yes, he ran toward Outer Drive."
Slowly, a crowd of people formed. The murmurs of the passersby replaced the quiet. All were curious, and asking the same questions.
"Who shot you?"
"Did he rob you?"
"Was it somebody you knew?"
Why would anyone do this to you?"
I had to interrupt the unofficial interrogation of me, "Will someone tell my parents that I am shot?" No one responded to my question. Nor did they think to call the police.
The sound of shots obviously aroused the neighborhood. Folks emptied their houses, either running to help or curious.
Then my mother arrived. Mom stroked my body to let me know she saw me, and abruptly turned around to call 911 for help.
"Probation officer shot! Mom said to the 911 operator. "We need an ambulance sent to my house immediately."
Next, my father came out of the house armed with a shotgun. He was going to maim the culprit who had done this to his baby. I couldn't help but notice that he walked like Arnold Schwarznegger, in *The Terminator*. He came over to me with a glazed look in his eyes and a fixed look of determination on his face. He wanted revenge.
I laid-back, resigned, saying, "Daddy, that man is long gone."
"Don't worry, sugar, I'll find him," he said.
Daddy ignored all that I said.

He then walked past me, still glassy-eyed and determined to settle the score with the fiend who invaded the sanctity of his castle and intruded on his turf. He needed to protect me from a faceless enemy. The shotgun gave him a sense of power. I was his offspring, the child who was his third-born of five. How did some stranger even think that he could come to his house and try to kill his daughter?

For 39 years my father planted good seeds in me. No stranger was going to try to erase it all in 60 seconds. My father seemed determined that night to find him. Nothing quenched Dad's anger. He wanted vengeance. My father was still trying to get over my husband's infidelity. Now another man was trying to hurt me too.

While on the cold, hard ground, I realized I needed to call the children and let them know that I was going to be late arriving home. At last, I tried to get up and walk to my parents' house.

"Denise. Stop and stay still!" You will move the bullets.

Debbie, a neighbor and a nurse, pushed her way through the crowd to aid me.

"Denise, you must lie still or else the bullets will move."

She compressed my stomach with her hands.

"Ouch, that hurts," I screamed.

"I'm so sorry—I have to push this hard to stop the internal bleeding. I don't want you to bleed to death."

Debbie took charge and shouted out orders.

"Somebody get a blanket. She needs to stay warm. I don't want her to go into shock."

Ann ran into her house and got a blanket.

Debbie wanted me comfortable. She hollered, "I need a pillow for her head." My mother went back inside the house and came back with one.

"Mom," I told her, "I need you to take care of my kids."

"Nise, don't worry, I will. You're my concern right now."

"Mom, I forgot to call Adam before I left work. Let him know that I won't be home tonight."

"You need to be still and stop worrying."

Kathy, Ann and Debbie continued helping me. Ann made me comfortable. She loosened my grip on my keys and money and covered me up so I wouldn't go into shock.

I wasn't Debbie's best patient that night. I complained the pressure was hurting. She eased up some. She was using all that she knew to try to keep me alive. The pillow made the half-hour wait tolerable.

Sirens wailed through the darkened night. More help arrived in the form of three police cruisers. As a probation officer, I was a comrade in distress. The police were like the cavalry arriving just in time to ward off a potential massacre—just like I had seen in my favorite wild west movies. I heard the screeching of tires and shuffling feet as they drew closer. The crowd opened a path for the blue uniforms. Kathy and Debbie's brother were answering questions.

Years later I learned the police handcuffed them as suspects. One officer said, "If she dies, we'll hold you both for murder. You better hope she pulls through."

They swarmed the area looking for the assailant, while one stayed behind. I thought he looked familiar. He came over and rubbed my forehead. It felt good; it eased my pain. I looked up at him. All I could see upside down was this big, black, fanlike mustache on a milk chocolate male face. I only knew one person who had such a noticeable mustache. Could this be Darnell Williams, a kid I'd known since middle school? He recently joined the police force, and I just wasn't sure. Anyway, he didn't move until the ambulance came.

The pain was like a fireball in my body, and sent hot flames throughout every part of me. My ears became sensitive to the noise from the crowd and all the questions. I decided I was not going to answer any more questions, so I pretended to go into shock. I stared straight up, fixed my eyes, and let my jaw drop open so I could breathe. I was, after all, shot. I didn't feel like chitchatting.

The pain was getting worse. The fifteen minutes on the cold ground seemed like hours. One police officer said, "The ambulance will arrive in 15 minutes. This news increased the throbbing in my head. I injured it when I fell.

Eventually, I heard sirens again. This time it was the ambulance. The technicians were quick and efficient. One person jumped out of the truck, even before it came to a screeching halt.

Someone in the crowd answered their questions about my injuries. They immediately strapped an oxygen mask on my face, which helped me to breathe easier. I didn't know then that a bullet had grazed my lungs. They rolled the gurney next to me, slid my body onto it and strapped me in.

"One, two, three—lift."

My saviors swooshed me into the truck and sped off. Mom had planned to ride in the ambulance with me. She went into the house to get her purse, but when she came out there were no signs of me anywhere. I said good-bye to no one.

One technician radioed the hospital.

"We have a gunshot victim, age 39, female, who suffered multiple gunshot wounds. Our estimated time of arrival is six minutes. Her vital signs are stable."

The trauma team was standing by, expecting my arrival. There were no familiar faces to gaze at for comfort. But I had skilled professionals doing their job, hoping to save my life.

The EMS technicians drove off to Grace Hospital; they were on a lifesaving mission. It was the worst six minutes I had ever experienced. While I was quietly internalizing the pain, I asked the attending technician for pain medication.

"I'm sorry, I'm not allowed to give you medication. It will put you in shock, and you will probably die."

It wasn't easy for him, either. The rocky ride irritated my injuries. For each bump, I screamed. The gurney slid backward and forward. I screamed louder and louder. My bullet-riddled body bounced unmercifully around in that ambulance. We must have found every chuckhole in the road during that five-mile ride. By now I lost any dignity or restraint from crying out.

"I can't take the pain. It hurts. It hurts. Please give me something for pain."

I screamed so hard the EMS technician cautioned me that I was just irritating the crisis.

"You'll increase your chances of surviving by staying as calm as you can, conserving oxygen and your strength."

He didn't know I was doing the best I could. With no pain medication, I was at the mercy of the increasing fire that mounted an attack on all my senses. Screaming was like letting the air out of an overblown balloon to keep it from bursting.

I don't know why his words were soothing, but they were. I stopped hollering, and sucked up more of the miracle air. I was trying to find relief from the pain and this was all they were offering.

6

The Skillful Scalpel

Fortunately for me, the hospital was close. The doors to the ambulance opened and the team was right there. The paramedics released me to the eagerly awaiting saviors who began their lifesaving protocol. Everyone played a role, and they were good at it. As the gurney rolled toward the emergency room, somebody or something examined almost every part of my body; they worked feverishly to save my life. It was like a scene from the television drama *ER*. Their faces were grim and the no-nonsense approach was breathless.

As I looked up from the crash cart, I saw a soothing smile from a familiar face. It was Peggy Taylor, from church. Fortunately for me, she worked there. The two of us worked together in the children's ministry. Daily, she saw many people burst through the doors, but seeing me surprised her. I thought she was an illusion. To make sure I was not in the early stages of shock, I sucked in more oxygen and with all the voice I could muster, I hollered, "Peggy, is that you?"

It was. She looked stunned, asking, "Denise, what happened? Does Pastor know you're here?"

"I don't think so."

I was rolled past her and into the emergency room. The doctor in charge asked many questions. While he talked, I watched the other team members undress me. One staff member cut off my clothes, including my new underwear. I wore a teal blue bra with matching panties—both of which coordinated with my teal blue, A-line dress. They cut it straight up the middle. I shuddered as I watched them destroy it. I took time to put that ensemble together, but minutes to ruin the memory. I also wore a beautiful teal blue scarf with white swirls. The nurse almost strangled me with it. She failed to see it attached to my neck. Once I gagged, she exercised more care and untied it. They yanked off my black leather boots, followed by my coffee-colored support panty hose. They left me there, naked.

So much for Mom's advice that we should always wear clean, decent underwear when we leave home, I thought.

"Denise," she'd say, "you never know when you may have an accident and in need of medical care. I don't want you kids embarrassing me with ragged underwear."

I realized then that Mom had no idea what hospitals do to decent underwear. They cut everything off! It didn't matter what I wore. It was in the way and they had to get it off in a hurry.

I had an IV tube in my arm, an X-ray machine on my stomach, and someone drew blood to find out my blood type. The doctor in charge talked about everything except when he was going to give me something for pain.

"Doc, could you give me something for the pain? Just a little bit would do. It would make answering questions easier."

"Not yet."

He talked and talked. It seemed like forever. That chatter irritated me, but it kept me alert. He asked my name. I said Denise but he heard Onise, and began calling me that name.

I hate it to have my name mispronounced. I reacted the way I do when someone screeches chalk or their fingernails across a blackboard. I clenched my teeth together. It increased my adrenaline—and my agitation—toward the doctor.

When he noted my irritation he said, indignantly, "We're trying to save your life."

"Sir, I know that, but I am not in the mood for chitchat. Please quit asking so many questions. I am having trouble breathing and in pain. I just want to go to sleep, so you guys can do what you need to do."

At last, we were on the same page. He called my name correctly. I signed for my surgery. We began working together.

Finally I met the anesthesiologist. He said, in his most soothing and caring voice, "I will be your anesthesiologist tonight. My job is to supply enough medication for the surgery. In just a few minutes I will put you out of your misery."

I liked his conversation.

With the preparations completed, the head surgeon alerted his team by hollering, "Let's take her to surgery."

Just then, I took a turn for the worse. I screamed as loud as I could, "I'm going to throw up."

A nurse quickly turned my head to the side, and placed a spittoon under my mouth. I started heaving up blood, followed by strong, painful, stomach spasms. My body lifted, as if shocked with defibrillators. Involuntarily, it lifted continuously. The doctor said, "She's bleeding internally. Let's get her to surgery."

Just as the drama intensified, I heard a familiar voice. Peggy again.

"Doc, she wants her pastor to pray for her before you begin."

He looked at me, and I nodded my head in affirmation.

The doctor said, "Get him in here, quick. We must get her to surgery."

I caught a glimpse of my pastor, Bishop David L. Ellis, leaning over me. He looked back at me with pain-filled eyes as he prepared to pray. I remembered this phrase, "Lord, please guide the surgeon's hands."

I wondered how he learned about the shooting. How did he know the right hospital? My sister-in-law, Chally, had called his wife, Wilma. She in turn called him on his cell phone and he sped off to the hospital.

I was just one of his many parishioners who had met with such violent battles. Emergency hospital runs came with his position as pastor. In fact, he told me later that he saw the EMS truck that took me to the hospital. When it passed him, a sense of urgency filled his heart, and he whispered a silent prayer, "God, please bless whoever is in that ambulance." He had no idea that it was me.

I never understood how he bore up under the strain of violence against his flock. Just a few weeks prior, two choir members miraculously survived a hit-and-run accident. A drunk driver hit both of them as they walked across Seven-Mile and Schaefer. The car knocked their bodies around like rag dolls. One was thrown 80 feet in the air and it crushed her leg. The other one landed on her face. It crushed facial bones and shattered her teeth. But her unborn baby survived.

Another member, a faithful usher, went home, after a Sunday morning service. His disgruntled spouse met him at the door. She aimed a shotgun at his head and blew it off. Bishop Ellis rushed to the scene. He identified the man by his usher's uniform that displayed the Greater Grace Temple emblem.

It was no small wonder that such a man of God prayed for me. I relaxed, knowing that God heard the prayer.

7

Potter's Touch

Before surgery, Dr. Salem, the head surgeon, gave an estimated time for surgery—five hours. Family, friends and folks from church kept pouring into the waiting room. Eventually everyone moved to a special waiting room.

Bishop Ellis gathered the crowd together and said, "We've got to pray for Denise. She needs our prayer. She needs a miracle. There are too many injuries for natural hands to fix."

After the prayer, they waited. The group consisted of some strange loyalties. My brother Darrell had his "boys" with him—and his girl-friend. His wife, Saun, was also present and shielded from disrespect by Bishop Ellis. My elementary school friend, Cheryl Hyatt, and her mother heard the incident televised on the evening news. The two of them rushed to the hospital to join the wait and make sure that I made it through.

My friend and prayer partner, Delorese, and her husband, Milton, came too. He learned before she did about the shooting. He prayed, "God, how am I going to tell my wife what happened?" God gave him the right words, and together they headed to the hospital to comfort the family.

Even Mortimer, my estranged husband, was there. He appointed himself the person in charge of the waiting room. A telephone was in the room, and whenever it rang, he answered. He told all callers about my progress. He acted like he cared. Mind you, this is the man who failed to express concern about me for nine months, who had replaced me with his new girlfriend.

A friend who lived in Florida told me she called the hospital and that Mortimer answered the telephone. It shocked her. My 31-year-old brother, Rex, confirmed her story and added to it. "I took charge. The first thing I did was get him off the telephone." I told him, "Look, Mortimer, get off the phone. As far as I'm concerned, you lost that right when you separated from my sister."

My friend, Crystal, and her husband lived only a few blocks from the hospital. When she heard the news, she began screaming. She later told me, "Jerry had to calm me down, and then drive me to the hospital. We joined everybody who prayed for you."

Of course all of my siblings were there, except Cheryl. She resides in Youngstown, Ohio. When she received the news, she stopped crying. That's right. She *stopped* crying.

Early that morning, God woke her up to pray. He gave her specific instructions. He mandated her to thank Him, in prayer, for every miracle, she knew He performed. It took her all-day to complete the task. She cried tears of thanksgiving. Just as she wiped the last tear away, the telephone rang. Chally called to tell her the dreaded news of the shooting. She wailed so loud that her husband thought she injured herself. While he tried to comfort her, God stepped in and whispered to her spirit, *"Now, add your sister, to the list."*

My brother, Butch, was there, too. He picked up Adam and Angie from my home and brought them to the hospital. When they entered the car, they saw a shotgun laying on the backseat. Originally, Butch told them that I was in a car accident. As they drove toward the hospital, they overheard his cell phone conversation describing the shooting. Angie began to cry.

Butch was upset because he thought Mortimer shot me. The car at the scene was a blue Topaz, similar to Mortimer's blue Tempo. He was gunning for him. I don't know what changed his mind, but he didn't use the gun that night. He and the children found their way to the hospital and joined the others in prayer.

Rex, my baby brother, took charge. As a member of several hospital boards, he knew people in prominent positions. Later, I learned, that he had used all his influence—both on Earth and in Heaven—to keep me alive.

He said, "Nise, staying busy kept me calm. I couldn't bare to think you might die."

Mom and Dad let him represent the family.

Of course, through all of this, I didn't know what was going on. I received a much-needed rest while the surgeons performed the surgery. The last words I heard came from Bishop Ellis praying, "God, guide the surgeon's hands."

My next memory came, when I woke up from the surgery. The recovery room nurse was checking my vital signs. I wiggled my toes and said, "I can wiggle my toes. I am not paralyzed. Did they get all the bullets?"

"Yes."

"Am I going to be fine?"

"Yes."

I kept talking a mile a minute. She smiled and said, "You've already asked that question a few times."

"I don't remember." I replied. "Was I talking under the anesthetic?"

"Yes," she giggled.

I was so glad to be alive and not paralyzed that I couldn't shut up.

While I was in recovery amusing the nurse, Dr. Salem talked to the family.

"Miraculously, none of the bullets went into any of her vital organs. The bullets that lodged in her right hip and tore up both colons gave her the biggest problem. We removed a section of the colon which was beyond repair." Then he added, "She's talking."

Someone said with comic relief, "Then she must be all right."

They all laughed. "She loves to talk.

Mom asked, "Could we see her?"

"Yes. I will allow the family to go in now. But please, stay only a few minutes. She needs her rest."

When they trooped into my room, they found all sorts of tubes sticking out of me. A huge, long tube down my throat into my stomach pumped out the excess bile. IVs were everywhere. There were little ones for antibiotics, bigger ones for antifungal solutions, one for glucose, saline, and other lifesaving fluids. An oxygen tube gave me the extra air to help my breathing.

Even with all the drama, I still failed to understand the seriousness of my medical condition.

8

Back in the Huddle of Love

I was moved from recovery to a regular room, once my vital signs stabilized. Dr. Salem gave my whole family a few minutes to visit with me. I needed to see them, and they needed to see me. I didn't know the whole city interceded for me in prayer. The news traveled fast. The major television stations reported the shooting.

Confusion set in when I heard that Mort was at the hospital. Perhaps he thought I would die, and he would get the life insurance money. However, neither one of us knew then that the marriage had been dissolved the day before. We hadn't received the final papers. We gave up our rights to any life insurance claims. It specifically annulled either one of us benefiting from the other's death.

Mortimer wanted permission to see me when the other family members visited. *Why was he there? I thought.* My last meeting with him was before the judge at the divorce hearing on November 25. So he surprised me when he came to the hospital. I'm sure my eyes bucked when he asked Rex to see me. I only consented to let him in with an escort.

"Don't leave me alone with him!" I said to Rex.

"I won't," said Rex "I will escort him myself."

Mortimer, escorted by Rex, said, "Do you remember long time ago you asked me this question: 'Can I depend on you in a crisis?'"

"Yes, I remember." I said.

"Well, I am here for you if you need me."

He was here for me? What did that mean? I couldn't believe this sudden change of heart.

"Thanks for coming," I said at last, looking puzzled as Rex who escorted Mortimer out of the room.

I can't remember all the faces, but after I greeted everyone they all went home. After they left, I reflected on my children's visit. I could see the pain in their eyes. My youngest child, Adam, couldn't control his emotions. At first the nurse wasn't going to let him in to see me, but my mother intervened.

"Please, nurse, let Adam see his mother. It will mean a great deal to him, and you can see he's already endured more than he can handle."

The nurse, at last, allowed Adam to see me. Once he was in the room big tears flooded his huge, sad, almond eyes and streamed down his face.

He told me later, "Mom, you didn't look like yourself. You had tubes everywhere and you were all swollen up. You didn't look like my mother who left home for work that day."

To this day the memory of that moment still stings his heart.

"How could they *not* let me see my mother?"

He remembers his grandmother interceding on his behalf. She was his champion that day. The mother that Aaron, Adam, and Angie thought of as strong and invincible was gone that night. The impersonator was vulnerable, and this new woman weighed in the balances between life-and-death.

After everyone left, I was alone with my thoughts. I survived the shooting, but what exactly would that mean for my future? *Would I be dependent on my parents for the rest of my life? Who would raise my children? Would it be Mortimer and his new girlfriend? Or could Saun handle the task?*

As I pondered these questions, my surgeon came in to see me. He entered my room, grinning like a Cheshire cat.

"Well, you're a lucky young woman on two counts. Those bullets didn't cause any lasting damage that we can predict. And we fixed a hernia that could give you trouble later. Wasn't it painful?"

"No," I replied, keeping it short.

I did not feel like talking. Nor could I find a smile that reflected my home training. I just wanted to go to sleep. I didn't get much of that during my first 24 hours in the hospital.

Every fifteen minutes the technicians took blood. My room was a revolving door for medical staff. I had a private room for security's sake, since this was protocol for all gunshot victims. The hospital did not want the unknown gunman to find me. They had already lost one patient that way. A few years before my shooting, a visitor killed a patient while he slept. The gunman came to the hospital and completed the job he originally botched up on the streets of Detroit.

9

Shadows of My Footsteps

I momentarily drifted off into a daydream. My mind began to wander through the events of 1992, the worst year I had ever lived. The first month, January, Mortimer, my husband, announced that he was leaving me.

"I love you as the mother of my three children, but I've had enough of you as a wife."

"Can't we work this out?" I cried. "Let's at least give counseling a try before throwing in the towel."

"No."

"For the sake of the children?" I groveled.

He softened, "I'll bear it a little longer."

March came in like an angry roaring lion, and Mortimer's firm resolve to leave was just as fierce.

"I'm leaving and that's it," he told me.

He told the children, "Your Dad's having a few personal problems, but nothing that God can't fix. There is no way I am leaving home."

But the next week, he began looking in the want ads for apartments to rent. Giving a promise and changing it without warning was typical of his character. It was obvious to me that separation was certain.

As I tried to make sense of what was happening, I wondered, what happened to the love we'd shared? Was it gone—just like that?

The sudden turn-around still caught me unprepared emotionally. He made his final announcement to the children while I was at church, performing as the mistress of ceremony for a prayer breakfast. While I prayed and ate, my children were at home with their father; struggling with the searing pain of impending loss.

I learned later that Adam sat there unsure what the announcement meant. Was he still going to play baseball and get his allowance? He did not want his routine interrupted. He wanted to continue enjoying life, as he knew it.

When I arrived home that day, I heard Angela's protest, "No, Daddy, you can't go!" Tears streaming down her cheeks and gasping for air, she went sobbing to her room to nurse her hurt. After all, she loved her daddy.

"Angela?" I whispered, opening the door to her room. I heard her muffled sobs.

"Angela?" I whispered again. "It's Mom."

She lifted her face from the pillow.

"Oh, Mom, *why?*"

I sat down on the edge of the bed and hugged her warmly.

"Daddy's going through some changes and needs to find himself."

She looked at me out of red-rimmed eyes.

"So...why can't he find himself living here?"

Why, indeed, I thought, sighing.

"Angie, sometimes adults have trouble living together, and have to live in two separate places. But listen to me, Angie, it doesn't stop them from loving their children."

But, we're not sure we still love each other, I thought.

At last, reassured that she would see her father regularly, and that I was the scapegoat for his leaving, not her, she calmed down. She was still his special girl.

He packed his bags and left. Obviously, he felt that abandoning his family was the cure to his midlife crisis. No more hours of sharing our love for the children together. In effect, he left me to raise our children alone. No more bible sessions where we shared the love of God's word together. Gone were the intimate talks and our shared love for God.

The children were the by-products of our love. He had loved us so much—what happened?

What I thought was a happy, sanctified, church-going family, headed by two ministers of the Gospel, was gone. The cold, icy, fingers of marital dysfunction and sin choked the life out of that picture.

Then in August, a week after Saun moved in, trouble knocked again. I fell on the steps, at the Waldorf Correction Center while returning house arrest equipment. Climbing upward with my purse slung over my shoulder, clipboard in my left hand, and the equipment in my right, I fell. Both feet slipped from underneath me—any tries to regain my balance were futile.

I heard the sickening sound of 250 pounds of flesh hitting the cement step, and cartilage breaking. Behind me was my mentor, Alonzo Grant. He and another coworker helped me up.

I stood up, brushing away their helping hands.

"Thanks, Alonzo."

"Did you hurt yourself?"

"Sure."

"You need to make an accident report."

Nodding my head, as if agreeing, was a ploy to leave without reporting the injury. However, before I could escape, Bernice Brown, the manager of the center, insisted that I file a report immediately. I didn't want to make waves, so I complied.

The constant reminders from falling, were my knees. They protested loudly as if betrayed by a trusted friend.

"How could you mistreat us like this? Haven't we given you faithful service? Is this how you repay our loyalty?"

For a week I struggled. Motrin and Tylenol both helped to ease the injured pair. Then, early Sunday morning, my chubby left knee looked like a balloon ready to pop. It was at least three times its normal size. I couldn't bend it. My dark chocolate knee was bright red, like a vine-ripened tomato. Something was wrong. Bless her soul, Saun took me to the emergency room at Harvey Studebaker West. The doctor diagnosed inflammation of the left knee.

He prescribed a few days rest, and anti-inflammatory medicine.

The next day my employer sent me to an industrial clinic for further medical help. Seven weeks of rehabilitation enabled me to return to work. However, Dr. Bledsoe, the orthopedic specialist, gave me an unwritten warning.

"Do not make any sudden movements when walking. Your left knee is unstable. If I keep you on a leave of absence much longer, your employer will force you to retire. I don't want to risk your future."

The injury had occurred during August's sizzling heat. Seven weeks later, everything had changed. I returned to work in October, during the height of autumn. The orange, red, and brown replaced the green landscape of summer. The confident woman, on the eve of turning 40, had lost her stride. Nothing was the same, including me.

10

Just the Facts, Please

On Wednesday, December 9, at 7:50 a.m., the day after the shooting, I needed to call my office. I wanted my supervisor, Grace Jackson, to know that I wasn't reporting for duty. I didn't want to assume she heard about the shooting. I needed to use my sick leave or vacation time to cover my absence. It was close to Christmas and needed all the money I could muster for presents. I didn't want my check altered because I had an unexplained absence.

My sister-in-law, Chally, a nurse by profession, stayed with me through the night. She helped me adjust to my new surroundings. She dialed the telephone number for me.

I could only whisper into the telephone.

"Hello, Grace, this is Denise. I've had an accident, and I'm sorry but I won't be in today."

She seemed surprised. "Why, Denise, I can't believe this. It just aired on the radio that you *died*. Alonzo Grant just called to tell us that you didn't survive the shooting. Oh, thank God, it wasn't true. Of course you won't be in today."

Then Grace said, "Denise, do you have enough strength to talk to Audrey? She's taking your shooting the hardest. She needs to hear your voice."

"I'll try," I told Grace. The receptionist connected me to Audrey. She had just lost her brother, through violence, and I had counseled her through her loss, a few weeks prior.

"Denise, I am so glad to hear your voice. I still don't believe it. I am praying for you. I want you to make a total recovery."

"Don't worry about me. I will be fine." I whispered.

After I hung up, my busy day began. Strangers came to visit.

Each one asked, "Do you remember me?"

Each played a role in my recovery, praying that I made it. Clearly, the visit was as much for their encouragement as it was for mine. The first was a tall, chocolate, African-American middle-aged man dressed in seafoam green scrubs. He was the anesthesiologist.

He smiled at me sheepishly and asked, "Do you know who I am?"

I looked at him and said, "No."

He said, "I'm the one who put you to sleep and put you out of your misery."

Embarrassed, I remembered how I had so often pleaded for a pain-killer.

"Thank you, oh, thank you. You did a good job," I whispered. "I'm glad you were there."

Another visitor came, the security guard, assigned to watch that no visitors came to my room, except those on a limited list. However, he was not in his uniform.

He noted the fear in my eyes, and he quickly identified himself.

He said, "I'm the security guard who was on duty when you arrived in emergency last night. I wanted to see if you were better. I'm not in uniform, because, today is my day off. I came to pick up my paycheck, so I thought I'd check on you."

He flashed a warm smile my way. He was charming. I wasn't too sedated to recognize a handsome, caramel, clean-cut man. It touched my heart that he cared.

I received many visits, like his, that day. Just as God said in prayer, *I was now receiving more love in my life than I had imagined.*

In the hospital, my routine consisted of tests, doctors, blood drawn, IVs, and official visits from the police department. I had a diagnostic X-ray screening for pneumonia, and dye injected through my groin, to see if I had any permanent damage to my legs, from the impact of the bullets. Temperature checks were constant.

While I adjusted to the hospital's antiseptic smell, and the machines' hisses and beeps, the stream of official visitors continued. Sergeant Parker, the officer in charge, was the first. He was a rugged type of man. His hair was wind blown. He seemed wired from too much coffee yet his eyes seemed wearied from too many cases. He looked like *Colombo* on television. Not a polished cop but knowledgeable. He knew his stuff. He talked and moved like he came from the streets, but his pale skin confirmed that he was a blue-eyed soul brother. Just as in the movies, as soon as I was able to talk the interrogation began. He was trying to get more details about what happened. I had to whisper around the tube in my throat that was extracting the green bile from my stomach. Sucking on the oxygen tube in my nostrils, I answered his questions.

"Can you identify the shooter?"

"Yes."

"The assailant shot you how many times?"

"Five."

"Where were you shot?"

"At my parents' house."

"He shot you where on your body"

"In the stomach."

"Did you see the weapon?"

"Sure did."

"What color was it?"

"Black."

"What model and make?"

"I am not sure. It is bigger than my .38 caliber pistol."

"Was the noise successive or one round at a time?"

"It shot like a machine gun."

I had some trouble describing the gun, so he pulled his gun from the holster. The shooter's gun looked like his, a black Glock 9-mm semiautomatic pistol.

"You were lucky that he didn't empty the whole clip into your belly. It holds 14 bullets," he said.

That was too much information for me. It made all the pains from the wounds worsen.

"Is it your statement the first bullet jammed? Then he tried again, clearing the jammed bullet out of the chamber so he could pump the remaining five bullets into your gut?"

"Yes," I said.

"Can you describe what happened?"

"Yes, I can,"

"How many people were with him?"

"Just him."

"Can you describe him for me?"

"Yes."

"Race?"

"African-American."

"How tall?"

"5' 11"

"How old?"

"Not sure. He was younger than me."

"Facial hair?"

"A mustache."

"Weight?"

"About 150 pounds."

"Complexion?"

"Milk chocolate."

"What was he wearing?"

"Army camouflage."

"Did he act alone?"

"Yes."

"Where were you shot?"

"I started out on my parents' driveway when I first faced the assailant. When I tried to back away from him, I backed onto the grassy knoll of the next door neighbors' property."

"Refresh my memory, how many times were you shot?"

"Five."

He looked for inconsistencies in my answers. Didn't he already ask some of these questions before?

"What are the injuries?"

"Both colons damaged. The doctors patched one and re-sectioned another. I have two bullet wounds on my left forearm, I don't remember him shooting me there, only in my stomach. My right groin hurts and my left elbow was scraped. When I fell backwards, I hit my head on the curb."

"What time of day was it?"

"Dusk."

"Why were you in the neighborhood?"

"Visiting my parents."

"Were you able to see?"

"Yes."

"Was it well lit?"

"Yes."

"Was it your ex-husband?"

"No."

"Would he have any reason to harm you?"

"No. Mortimer is a mild-mannered guy. This doesn't match his personality."

Questions, questions, questions, all to help them find the man who shot me. Throughout the ordeal, I had to give these same answers over and again. It was exhausting. There were so many people inquiring about the facts surrounding this case that a hospital staff member asked me, "Who are you, Miss? People are flooding our switchboard. What do you do?"

I learned later that my employer was trying to decide the facts. In case I didn't recover, they needed to know if it was a duty-related incident. The time was important for Worker's Compensation. If killed in the line of duty, a federal law mandated my employer to pay twice my salary to my estate, plus my life insurance benefits.

Also, the Department of Corrections was trying to manage the media spin on the facts. They would have received a grade of D, from me, for their fact gathering. I read at least one memo that had false information. It looked like a well-crafted story from a creative writing class.

Finding the truth was difficult. I'm not sure who their source was, but it couldn't have been the police. At least the Detroit police's information was almost correct. What I said and what people wrote didn't match. I'm glad that I had family present most of the time to corroborate what I was saying.

Next, I had my first experience with a police artist. He used a recipe box of facial features to put together a composite, but the box wasn't complete. I had trouble finding the right mustache for his face. The box limited my choices for African-American features. Overall, he did a decent job and it was real enough to stir up emotions inside me. The police department circulated the composite of the suspect to the media. My family posted a $5,000 reward for information that would lead to the arrest and conviction of the assailant.

11

Hugs and Kisses

I had a restricted visitor's list. Even close relatives weren't on the list. The list excluded most friends and coworkers. My pastor told my church family, about 2,500 members, not to visit. Their job was to pray. Even those who had visiting privileges had trouble finding me. For my protection, the patient information registry removed my name.

When Elder Charles Ellis, the administrative assistant and my pastor's son came to see me, he had to walk the halls until he found me. He cheered my soul. He prayed and made me laugh with his humor. He encouraged me, assuring me before he left that God was going to bring me out.

Elder Kevin Harrison, an old friend, found a way to visit me in the hospital. He and his family had moved to Thomasville, Georgia, a few months prior. He heard what happened to me and made it his mission to find a way to see me.

I was so surprised when he eased into my room, unnoticed at first. Once I recognized his presence, he smiled.

"How did you get in here?" I asked. "Only those approved by the family can visit!"

"You know with clergy credentials I can cut through the red tape."

"You came to see about me?" I smiled.

"Your well-being concerned me before I left to accept the position of pastor, in Thomasville. Debbie and I were heartbroken to hear what happened to you. It wasn't Mort was it?"

"No," I said.

"Why would anyone do this to you?"

"I don't know."

"Listen, before I am discovered let me pray for your speedy recovery."

All I could do while he prayed was to smile with an occasional giggle. I loved him like a brother. I missed his whole family. Their absence left a void inside me. It was a much-needed visit.

His wife, Debbie, and I had one eventful birth experience at the same time. We vowed to birth our children on the same day. I delivered first. I took castor oil that sped up my labor pains. I delivered a day before her—really only about twelve hours before. She birthed Kevin Jr., and I birthed Angie. We were at the same hospital, on the same floor. We had a great time. We visited in each other's rooms day and night. We were the delight of the nurses. If it was pill time, they knew where to bring our medication. This experience brought our families closer. It warmed my heart to see him. Our friendship had endured our hard times.

Reverend Clarence Crews, a probation officer, also visited me. He stayed briefly and prayed for my healing. Sister Bobby Brooks, who was on my children's church staff, was a hospital employee working in food service. Once I began eating, she would deliver my tray daily. She'd combed my hair and brought gum to take away the bile taste in my mouth.

People continued to find me, some by accident and some by deliberate strategy. Deborah, also a children's ministry worker, prayed to see me. The report of my recovery didn't satisfy her aching heart. She prayed for a chance meeting with me. Then one day my doctor ordered an angiogram of my legs, her doctor ordered an x-ray of her foot, and we met in radiology. Was it chance or a divine intervention?

As I lie on the gurney in the hallway, I saw her walk by. I couldn't call too loudly, but it was enough for her to hear me. She saw me and smothered me with greetings and kisses.

She said, "You're an answer to my prayers. I asked God to let me see you."

I didn't know at the time that she was going through some major podiatry problems. God has healed us both.

Cheryl didn't arrive until the Thursday following the shooting. She was deathly afraid to fly, but she came anyway. She arrived with a bottle of blessed oil and declared, "Nisey, I'm going to anoint you in the name of Jesus."

She wasn't on the list of visitors initially, but after a confrontation with Rex, she overrode his protest and found me. Not only did she visit, but also spent the night. As Cheryl and others prayed for me, I experienced a much-needed sensation of peace.

Someone had to coordinate my care while I was in the hospital, so my youngest brother, Rex, took charge. At the time, Rex was a Director of Community Relations and Player Programs for the Detroit Pistons Basketball Team.

It was his job to coordinate projects, and I was his project. When I looked uncomfortable, he made sure he addressed it. I had trouble eating. Only apple juice agreed with my stomach, and the hospital ran out of apple juice. The dietician tried substituting pineapple juice, but it didn't work. Rex went to the head of dietary services to discuss the matter. She allowed my family to bring juice from home and house it in the staff refrigerator. This adjustment hastened my recovery. It even helped me to gain favor with the staff. I drank apple juice whenever I needed it.

My parents told me that Rex was doing everything he could to keep me alive. I appreciated his loving care.

As I mentioned before, my father was preparing to retire. A retirement dinner in his honor was scheduled, but he didn't want to celebrate.

"I've decided not to go, Denise. I don't feel like celebrating." My father said.

"But, Dad, I want you to go. After over thirty years with the federal government, it would be a shame to leave without giving your staff and colleagues a chance to say good-bye."

At last, after my urging, he went. Mom had retired seven months prior. Both were in need of a rest when my crisis occurred. However, they didn't miss a day at my bedside. Both tried to wear the cheeriest smiles they could muster. They put on a good show, but I could see their worried faces.

I began showing signs of pneumonia. The doctors encouraged me to walk to stop it from getting worse. When I was able, I walked. My parents were my walking partners. No matter how they felt. One day, fatigue and worry were overtaking my mother. She walked up the stairs as usual instead of taking the elevator, and then to my room. When she arrived, she was too tired to walk any farther.

"Nise, I can't walk with you today."

"Mom, that's okay, I am just glad to see you."

But fifteen minutes into the visit she said, "Let's go."

"Go where?" I asked.

"Walking." She said, as if I needed a reminder.

Off we went, down one hall and up the other. Mom had found strength from somewhere and she never missed a day. She walked with me until I was well enough to walk right out of the hospital.

Dad was about the same. He had a week left before he officially quit work, but ended his career a few days early so he could be at the hospital as often as possible. He needed to hear that I was going to be all right. Sometimes he accompanied my mother, other times he came alone. He kept watch as though he were making sure that no one could try again to hurt me.

12

Reality Check Up

For the first few days after the shooting, I was on heavy-duty medications and my mind was a little hazy. In my dreams I relived my body going into spasms, just as it did before I went into surgery. I'd awake in terror after every nap and push the panic button, hoping the nurse would help me out of this problem.

A male African nurse usually responded to my panic call, since it happened most often on his midnight shift. It took his comforting words to convince me that I was dreaming.

In a heavy, foreign accent, he said, "Seemed real, huh? It was just a dream."

He'd hold my hand and pat it until I was calm.

"I'm sorry," I said, "I thought it was happening. I don't mean to be a pest."

"Nonsense, that's why we're here. You're not a bother."

This scene repeated itself over and again. In my nightmare, my body would leap up from the gurney. I would throw up streams of blood, followed by nausea, worse than morning sickness. However, a new part was added: pain and fear followed the nausea.

I decided that if I didn't go to sleep I could avoid the dream, so for two days I fought going to sleep. On the second day of no sleep, I was delirious. I imagined the biblical figure Job was a visitor in my room. I asked him some questions about his ordeal and learned that he was more understanding about *his* ordeal than I was about mine.

In my hazy mental state, I started having conversations with Job as if he were my roommate.

"Man, I never understood what you went through. It was more of a story than a real-life event. Surely, no one could have survived what you experienced. I want you to know that I wasn't as compassionate about your pain as I should have been. Will you forgive me for my indifference?"

I don't know if he answered or not. Somewhere in my head I believed he was listening.

"If you made it, I know I can, too—with God's help."

Something about his faith in God's ability to protect him gave me comfort. From that day until freed from the hospital, I talked with him daily.

"Man, how did you feel when your friends said you caused your own problem? Where did you find those friends? How did you find the strength to pray for them?" I asked.

I had my parents bring my Bible so I could read the story of Job. Then I found that my vision was too blurry to read it, so I had to entertain myself with my own account of the story:

Job was a good man, loved and favored by God. This man would have won the Citizen of the Year Award, if such an honor had been available. He was active in the community, remembered the poor, and met their needs. His neighbors and friends were glad to have him around. Then, one day, the angels and Satan went before God.

God singled out Satan and asked, "Satan, where have you been?"

He answered, "I've been traveling throughout the Earth."

God said, "Have you seen My servant, Job?"

"Who?"

"Job."

Satan scowled. "Oh, I looked at him, but you built a hedge so high around him that I can't get to him. He wouldn't be faithful if you removed that hedge."

"You think so? You don't know him, then."

"He only serves You because You give him everything he wants or could imagine, and You shower him with wealth, children and a good marriage. It isn't hard for him to serve You under those conditions. If I had the chance, I'd cause him to curse You and turn away."

God said, "Go ahead, touch what belongs to him. Your permission is conditional. You cannot and will not touch his soul. He will successfully endure the test. I know him."

"Well, I'll show You that Mr. Goody Two-Shoes won't survive. I will do him like I did Adam and Eve. They were Your pride and joy, but they disobeyed. See you later, God."

The testing started immediately. His cattle stolen, his children killed, his health gone, friends falsely accused him of sinning, and his wife told him to curse God and die. Mrs. Job hated his troubles. At least if he died, she could start again. She mourned the death of her children, her lifestyle, and her connection with Job. Her husband's influence in the community determined her status. His sickness left them pitied instead of honored.

However, even though his body was decaying and wracked with pain, he did not stop believing in the truthfulness of his God. Job loved his agreement with God. God promised never to leave him or abandon him. He had no guarantee that his circumstances would change for the better, but he was sure of God's love.

Job said, *Though he slay me, yet will I trust in him: but I will preserve mine own ways before him.* (Job 1:15)

Job survived. Not only that, God doubled his blessings when he prayed for his miserable friends. He survived and so would I. This wasn't the only revelation I learned from Job, but it was a place to begin.

Job had to learn how to keep his faith despite his circumstances, and to do it when he had no support from his loved ones. He learned that trusting in God could sometimes be a lonely walk.

Others accused Job of sinning. He learned that when others couldn't make sense of his problems, they looked for someone or something to blame. They did this to make their own conscience feel better and calm their own fears.

To be blamed for his troubles was cruel and unusual punishment, especially during a time when Job needed comfort. He preserved his connection with God, and did not falter because of the weight of his circumstances.

Neither his wife nor his friends understood him. Job showed faith in action. True, in his humanity, Job didn't understand why this happened to him, but to his credit he continued to believe God.

I believe Satan and his imps were having a ball, laughing at Job.

"Where's your God now, Job?" Laughed one imp of destruction.

"Your kids are gone. Your cattle gone. Your wife doesn't want you any more. She told you the other day to curse God and die. Why don't you listen? It would be the honorable way to end your life. Your neighbors are all talking about you. They say you must have sinned. Admit it, you did. You're self-righteous. You'd rather uphold your innocence than admit your guilt. You're already a dead man. Give up and accept it. Help God out and do everyone around you a favor, take your own life."

Those accusations sounded familiar. Those same words echoed through my mind regularly. Wasn't that just like the accusers of our souls? Satan and his imps always trying to discredit us. Lies woven from facts crafted so skillful that even an honest man could yield. His wife and friends believed he caused the problems. Their yielding to the lie opened a door for doubt. However, Job stood steady with hope.

Job replied, "The Lord giveth and the Lord taketh away; blessed be the name of the Lord."

That was an exceptional response from a man who lost his ten children, all his possessions, his health, and his good standing in the community. Bless Job; he gave me hope amid my own dark times.

The recurring nightmares and hallucinations were reasons for medical concern. Mom made a call to my marriage counselor, Dr. Laverne Poindexter. She told Mom that a psychiatric referral was in order. It was possible that I could experience such flashbacks for years to come. My reaction was a common side effect.

The hallucinations and nightmares weren't my only problem. By the fourth day, I felt better. As I filled out the menu, I watched the Gospel programming on the television.

I was singing with the singers, enjoying the message of encouragement, and so engrossed in filling out the menu that I didn't realize the movie *Twelve O'Clock High* was on.

Then I heard the roaring of airplanes and a gun battle. *POW, POW, POW*—I was back on Sorrento Street, shot again. I tried to turn off the television, but couldn't.

The nurse made my bed and pushed the remote out of her way. She failed to place it within arms reach of my bed. The tubes restricted me, so I couldn't turn the television off.

I thought, *Oh no, someone is shooting at me again.* I began hollering. "Help! Somebody help me!"

At first no one heard my cry. I was sure that I was going to die before someone found me. Just when I was in a full-blown panic, Dr. Spencer Vincent walked in. He was a colleague of a church member, Dr. Vickie Rohns. She had asked him to watch out for me, since he was on staff. He usually visited early every morning. This day was different; he was late.

He asked, "What's wrong?"

"I heard shooting," I said.

In a low, soothing tone he said, "You felt afraid?"

"Yes."

"Are you reliving the shooting all again?"

"Yes."

"You are not alone. I am here."

"Thank God!"

"I won't let anything happen to you."

"Are you sure?"

"I haven't yet. I check on you every day, don't I?"

"Yes."

"Did I today?"

"Yes."

"If you need me, just have them page me. All right?"

"Sure."

I calmed down eventually and later went to sleep exhausted. Up to that point, I was still in denial about my wounds being life threatening. Several days later, I experienced a more serious hysteria.

"Why did someone want me dead?" I sobbed. "What did I do to make someone want to kill me? I'm a good person. Why did this have to happen to me? He could have killed me."

I was chanting about how unfair this all had been. I realized that I could have died. I requested visits from the chaplains and the social workers. I finally realized that someone had tried to kill me. I wasn't easy to console. I wanted answers that no one could give me.

The chaplains used scriptures, and the social worker used crisis intervention tools to try to bring rest to my vexed spirit. I needed around-the-clock supervision. The social worker, psychiatrist and day chaplain checked on me during the day. The night chaplains visited me during the evening. They made sure that I never felt alone again.

13

Good News of the Gospel

I drew deeply on my knowledge of God during this ordeal. I felt scrambled. My senses—screwed up. My safety—gone. My memory of God and the Gospel of Jesus Christ rehearsed in my head daily just so I could hold onto my sanity.

The book of John helped to reassure me that I was not alone. I tried to remember my Bible class lessons that taught about God sending comfort in times of trouble. I needed all the comfort I could find.

Jesus stated in the book of John that he would send back a Comforter from Heaven once He left from this Earth. He knew that frail human beings, like me, needed help. I needed that Comforter during my recovery. Someone to walk me through the rough times.

The Holy Spirit is the Comforter. Bishop Ellis taught that the Comforter would be with me always after I accepted Jesus Christ as my personal Savior. John 14:26 reads, *"But the Comforter, which is the Holy Ghost, whom the Father will send in my name, he shall teach you all things, and bring all things to your remembrance, whatsoever I have said unto you."*

John 14:12 says, *"Verily, verily, I say unto you, He that believeth on me, the works that I do shall he do also; and greater works than these shall he do; because I go unto my Father."*

In other words, Christ healed the sick. Me too. He delivered the oppressed. Me, too. He raised the dead. Me, too. He sent back the same resurrection power that raised Christ from the dead. All believers have this power through the Holy Spirit. Until my hospital stay, those were just words. I misunderstood the power I had to heal from within.

Jesus said in John 14:16, *"And I will pray the Father, and he shall give you another Comforter, that he may abide with you forever."*

Sometime after the first four days, the constant presence of the Comforter became apparent.

John 15:26 says, *"But when the Comforter is come, whom I will send unto you from the Father, even the Spirit of truth, which proceedeth from the Father, he shall testify of me."*

John 16:7 says, *"Nevertheless I tell you the truth; It is expedient for you that I go away: for if I go not away, the Comforter will not come unto you; but if I depart, I will send him unto you."*

As I pondered these Scriptures, the Comforter met me in that room and began working in my body. My speedy recovery amazed my doctors.

John 14:17 *Even the Spirit of truth; whom the world cannot receive, because it seeth him not, neither knoweth him: but ye know him; for he dwelleth with you, and shall be in you.*

Right before my eyes my skin healed. The wounds on my arm were healing so fast that they took the gauze off and began using those veins to draw blood. This was unusual, since the protocol for such injuries would have been to avoid that area.

After a few days I began walking the hall with my IV bottle on a pole. When I escaped from the privacy of my room, I felt better. I walked and talked with other patients. I found one woman who told me she dropped dead from a massive heart attack. She credited her survival to the speedy work of the paramedics.

I told her, "They helped, but God gave you life. May I pray for you?"

She agreed, so I placed my hands on her forehead and prayed for her total recovery.

The next day she saw me and said, "Thanks for the prayer. It worked. I'm leaving today."

A friend from church, Mother Rogers, was on the same floor that I was on. I wasn't sure that I had permission to be in her room, so one day I quietly eased into her room, put my hands on her feet, and prayed for her healing while she was asleep. Once finished, I eased back out unnoticed. Her doctor released her the next day. That pattern continued until all my new acquaintances were gone. It was getting lonely, and I wanted to leave, too.

This new revelation of the power of the Comforter caused me to want to share it. I called Bishop David Ellis, who didn't have a clue what I was talking about.

I said, "I am watching my arm heal before my eyes."

He said, "That's good."

"You don't understand. The Holy Ghost is more than speaking in tongues. He can heal injuries. I am seeing it with my own eyes."

He may not have gotten it that day. He understood something unusual happened when the doctors released me after only twelve days.

14

Face to Face with Fear

Twelve days were all that I needed in the hospital. This puzzled the doctors.

One doctor said "We can't think of any reason to keep you, so we will, reluctantly, let you go. If you have any problems, don't hesitate to return."

Mom quickly retorted, "She won't be back."

Medically, there was nothing more they could do. It was up to God for a total recovery. Equipped with home-care instructions, a fist full of prescriptions, and my newfound faith in God, I left the hospital.

I didn't go to my home. My parents insisted that they were the care-givers. This meant that I had to face the scene of the crime again, which left me feeling uneasy.

How will I feel when I see the spot where he shot me?

I kept my reservations within. On arrival, my father escorted me through the door with a shotgun drawn for my protection. That is how it was!

My father wasn't sure I was safe when I went through his door, so he drew his shotgun every time I went in and out. Daddy's diligence assured me that I was safe. It was a little nerve-racking at first, but I endured. I was looking forward to returning to my home, where a shotgun escort wasn't needed.

While I was in the hospital, someone threw a brick into my parents' next-door neighbor's picture window. It was on his grass where I had fallen when shot. My family thought the perpetrator might have come back to harass my family and me, but gotten the wrong house.

Fear gripped the neighborhood. No one understood the violence. When would it end? Was it safe to resume a daily routine without fear? The shooting changed everyone.

Once we were safe inside, Mom worked at nursing me back to good health. Both she and my father took care of me as if their lives depended on it. I saw the strain from the wear and tear, but they never complained.

At their home, I received many visitors. One was the police officer that massaged my head at the scene, my old friend, Darnell, who had gone to school with me.

He said, "I told the other officers to hunt for the shooter, because I wanted to stay with you until the ambulance came. Do you know what I was doing when I was rubbing your head?"

Before I could answer, he told me, "I was praying."

"Thanks," I said. "I needed all the prayer that I could get. Your rubbing my forehead kept me calm.

I went on to tell him the details of the shooting, as I knew them.

"Darnell, the gunman targeted my chest, originally. Thank God, I fell. He changed his aim and pointed the gun at my stomach. I didn't want to die like that; another homicide statistic."

"I hear about murder everyday. People die from one bullet. Very few survive five. You are one blessed woman."

Darnell's familiar face that night was a blessing from God. It lessened the pain. Although I experienced much anguish, his smile made it bearable.

"Was your attacker one of your clients, past or present?" Darnell asked.

I pondered the often-asked question and answered. "No, he didn't look familiar. I'm not even sure of his motive. I assumed it was a robbery, but he didn't try to take anything from me. Anyway, my rapport with my clients is great. I doubt if anybody would want me dead."

Perhaps I was in denial.

15

Media Scoop

Teresa Tomeo, from Channel 50 News, performed my first television interview.

She asked me, "To what do you credit your still being alive?"

I answered, "God. I am a miracle."

When this interview aired, my acquaintances and friends breathed a sign of relief. Most of them worried about my well being. The broadcast allowed them to see me for themselves. My skin was pale, and my speech slow, but I still appeared strong.

"Wounded Officer Leaves Hospital," read the caption of the newspaper article, written by Roger Chesley, for the Detroit Free Press. The words he wrote seemed unreal to me.

As I read about that terrible day, December 8, I asked God,

"How did You let this happen to me?"

The next paragraph said, "As a probation tether agent for the Department of Corrections, Denise Thomason, regularly keeps tabs on at least 40 felons, in [Aspen] County."

He's talking about me, I thought.

I read further, "But Thomason, 39, never thought she'd be a crime victim herself. And she's thankful to be alive."

Everything seems like a nightmare; at anytime I'll wake up.

It really happened. Mine was one of the many violent crimes that year. Deaths, drive-by shootings, car jackings, and drug wars were all common headline topics in 1992. My hometown, once fondly known as, "The Motor City," was full of violence. That year Detroit, earned a new nickname: "The Murder Capital of the World." My city became a war zone. Deaths by murder rose to 586. I almost became number 587.

The media helped to find the perpetrator. A police composite circulated over the airways. Huel Perkins, on Channel 2, aired the story and announced the $5,000 reward, offered by my family, for the arrest and conviction of the assailant.

The Detroit News and *The Detroit Free Press* sent reporters to scoop the facts. I needed their help.

A local media Christian celebrity, Reverend Glenn Plummer, the president of the Christian Television Network, gave exposure to my story. He saw my testimony on the Greater Grace Temple's weekly television broadcast, and wanted to interview me as his guest. In January 1993 our church secretary, Mrs. Horne, called my house.

"Denise, Reverend Glenn Plummer, from the Christian Television Network, wants permission to call you. He heard your story and wants you to be a guest on his broadcast."

"Wow, what an opportunity," I said, "I watch his broadcast all the time. Mrs. Horne, give him my permission to call."

The details are rather fuzzy now. I believe someone from his network called me and I consented to give an interview. It took only one week to finalize the arrangements. I told my story to both Reverend Plummer and his assistant. Both of them were eager to interview me. I rehearsed the same information that I shared with my church at the New Year's Eve service. He found it amazing that I survived such a violent ordeal. His humble interviewing style put my fears at rest. He gave me a unique opportunity to tell about God's miraculous power. After the interview, I was strengthened in my faith in God, to take one more step towards recovery.

16

Hands of Mercy

The doctors released me from the hospital just in time. The family, almost out of energy, needed some relief. Unfortunately, that was just the start of my recovery. First, I needed to regain an appetite. I could only eat about a tablespoon of food at one setting.

Mom became worried, so Dad decided he'd cook a meal for me. He used all the wrong ingredients. He fried sausage and eggs, and made grits and toast with margarine. Greasy foods nauseated me. Surprisingly, I ate everything without getting sick!

Bishop Ellis visited my parents' house to get a private update.

"Evangelist Denise, how are you doing?" he asked.

"Bishop, I am having trouble eating. I tolerate about one tablespoon of food at each meal." I said.

"Let me pray. Nothing is impossible with God."

He prayed for me and left. I've been eating well since then. Probably too well.

My middle brother, Darrell, served as one of my bodyguards. He and his girlfriend had the necessary armory to keep me out of harm's way. Darrell kept his pistol in his shoulder holster and his girlfriend, Gail, kept her pistol in her purse.

My oldest brother, Butch, visited during the day between business calls. If I had a financial problem, or needed a ride to the doctor, he was at my disposal.

"Denise, just let me know what you want to do. You know I will find a way to help." Said Butch.

"I need to get some air. You have to find a way to get me out of the house without Mama or Daddy suspecting any thing. If they get wind, of what we are doing, they are not going to let me go." I whined.

While recuperating, Dr. Kerner scheduled many medical appointments. I saw a psychologist. I needed a CAT scan, and more X-rays of my hip. The clotted blood obscured an accurate reading of the hip x-ray. Therefore, Dr. Kerner could not see what damage had been done to the hip. She knew it wasn't operating correctly, so she decided to send me to physical therapy. I could not drive myself to the sessions because the bullet that struck my right hip had disabled my right foot. It would not obey commands. I dragged it along when I walked. I wondered, *is it disconnected from my brain?*

My doctor referred me to physical therapy. The physical therapist helped me to do exercises to retrain the brain. At first, it wasted my time. Session after session, I would drag my right side into the work area. I left discouraged. Maimed, I couldn't believe it. Was this new challenge my fate? I hoped not. I needed strong healthy legs to keep my job. *What was I going to do now?*

Back in August, seven weeks of physical therapy had mended my knees so I could return to work. I didn't expect to be back in physical therapy so soon.

One day, Butch was my driver. He asked, "What do you want to do?"

I said, "Let's get some pizza."

So he and I went to Buddy's Pizzeria. We got in trouble that day because we failed to tell the family. We just disappeared and had a good time. We laughed and joked about silly stuff. I needed some humor, and Butch was the right person for the job. Since childhood he has clowned, and God used him as my comic relief. He often came and busted me out of the prison of hopelessness. I valued his efforts and love.

Getting shot at Christmastime was a bummer. Everyone was scurrying around buying gifts and going to dinner parties. I was fighting for my life. My immediate goal was to be well enough to see Christmas Day.

My children were in the care of their overwhelmed Aunt Saun. The new responsibilities challenged her. She was still afraid that I might die. Angela was not responding well to her authority. Angela wanted to go to the mall with her friends, and Saun told her no.

Angie replied, "Look, I'm not going to put my life on hold just because that man shot my mother."

This statement pierced my soul like a knife, when Saun repeated it to me. Nearly twelve years later, Angie explained where the statement originated. The morning after the shooting her aunt made that statement to persuade Angie to go to school. She obeyed her and went, but didn't like the decision. Later when Angie wanted to go to the mall, Aunt Saun said, "No." Angie used it to get her way. It backfired. Angie, thinking like a thirteen-year-old, wanted her aunt to hear how ridiculous it sounded. All it did was get her in trouble.

I was eager to go home and take care of the children myself. I also wanted to go Christmas shopping so they wouldn't miss Christmas, too.

That was the first Christmas of their lives that their father would not celebrate at home with us. I had planned to make it as happy as possible. With me struggling to survive that Christmas was not quite the image I had for our celebration. With our nuclear family torn apart, I wanted to make it as normal as possible.

My parents agreed to shop for their gifts. I received many cards and monetary donations, plus a Christmas check from my union. We needed the help.

There was, however, another desperate need—a new mattress and box spring. At my parents' home, I slept on a soothing waterbed. At my house, I would return to a box spring broken in the middle. I really needed a new mattress set. This defect caused me to roll down into a hole, surrounded by mattress. It made me into a human sandwich: I was the meat between both sides of the mattress. I needed a mattress to speed up my body's recovery. With twenty-five staples in my stomach rolling hurt. With all the generous donations, I was able to buy a new Sealy Posturepedic pillow top mattress.

That year, Christmas was a celebration of thankfulness.

Dad said, "*You* are our Christmas present. We need to put a ribbon on you."

It made me feel special. One of my gifts that year was a fluffy, pink bear. I loved it and when life became unbearable, I would hug it for comfort.

My children couldn't understand why I was so determined to get them gifts. They wanted me to concentrate on getting well so I could go home, but I needed to give gifts of love so I could feel the warmth in my heart instead of the worry that already invaded almost every crevice. A real mother doesn't stop looking out for her family until she draws her last breath. Only death was going to stop my concern. I enjoyed being a mom, and five bullets weren't going to change that.

My coworkers were great. They knew I was low on sick leave and tried to see if they could give theirs to keep me going, but that was not possible.

Among the cards and letters was an especially touching one from my girlfriend, Delorese. She sent me a letter dated December 14, 1992:

My Dear Friend Denise,

His love is just like an ocean, it shall never run dry. His love is just like a mountain—it will stand the test of time, as endless as the heavens, so deep and wide, his love so divine.

My soul went down to the deepest despair when I heard what had happened to you and you are yet not out of my thoughts because of your suffering. I rejoice in the Great God that we serve continually for sparing your life. Great is His Faithfulness. He chose His beloved to suffer for His glory. What great things we are expecting to see God manifest in your life and family....God...faileth not and worketh ALL things to our good.

Denise, although I cannot take away the pain that you now suffer, may your heart and spirit be encouraged, for a better day lies ahead. A day of victory, for He allowed this suffering to occur that he might turn the oppressed to Him, lift the brokenhearted, and set at liberty they that are in bondage, strengthen the weak, and lift heads that hang down. God will surely use your ministry in a great way. So you MUST continue to write your book and I will help you in any way that I can.

I love you Denise…and I am so grateful that God has spared me from the deepest despair. You could now be in a far better place than here, but God said your work is not yet done.

Your beloved friend,

Delorese.

Christmas that year was a celebration of life—it was one of the most memorable ones that I have experienced. To make it even better, my children came over and celebrated it with me.

17

New Year's Eve Praise Party

I made up my mind that 1993 had to be a better year than 1992, and I wanted to celebrate in the Watch Night Services at church. Greater Grace Temple Detroit was the place to be on New Year's Eve. We knew how to welcome in a New Year. Although I looked forward to seeing everyone, my parents weren't. They thought it was still too soon to be mingling in public. Finally, they agreed I could go.

I needed escorts. Darrell and his girlfriend Gail continued as my armed bodyguards. He still strapped a gun to his shoulder and she still carried one in her purse. Neither was afraid to use a gun if it came to that. Darrell had a license to carry a hidden weapon for his business.

Imagine this, the door opens at my parents' and Dad stands by with a loaded shotgun while I get into the car with my bodyguards. On arriving at church, they walked close to me. I moved swiftly through the door to the pulpit area assigned for the clergy. My guardians sat only a few feet away. Trouble didn't have a chance with these two sharpshooters behind me. Too much prayer was in that place for harm to find me that night.

I was "loved on" with gentle hugs, kisses, surprised giggles, and laughter. My friends told me that Bishop Ellis had announced that I was coming to the service that night. His excitement was obvious when he saw me. The last time he had seen me was at Mom's, and I looked a little ghastly with big, dark circles around my eyes, and my speech was slow and weak.

That night I had color in my cheeks, and I had come in expectation of a celebration. It seemed as though it had been months, not weeks, since I was in church. Everyone looked so *good* to me. It was a special night.

Each Watch Night, Bishop Ellis gave the ministers time to say a few words. When it was my turn, a hush came over the congregation.

Bishop Ellis began by saying: "Many of you read your newspaper and watched the newscast by television. Recently, one of our own met a near-death experience, almost a misfortune, right in a neighboring area. I am so thankful that she is here. Sister Denise Thomason, come and give your testimony."

The Greater Grace Temple television cameras were running to tape my story of victory. At 10:50 p.m., as the old year was ticking away, the pastor's son, Minister Spencer Ellis, helped me out of my chair and ushered me to the podium. His father greeted me with a kiss and left me at the microphone while he took his seat.

The theme of the service was "Thanksgiving." The choir sang the song "Thank You", my favorite. That night, the congregation favored it, too. The church exploded with dancing, shouting, clapping and singing. We had a genuine, sanctified party.

That night the lyrics to the song gave birth in my soul, "*I could have been dead, lying in my grave….*" Before that night those were just words in a song, but that evening they became part of my story.

"Praise the Lord, everybody. I'm so glad that I'm able to say, 'Praise the Lord.' If the devil had had his way, I wouldn't be here to say it," I exclaimed.

Deafening claps and cheers exploded from the crowd. It felt as good to hear the cheers as if I had been a soldier, wounded in battle, returning home from the war.

I went on: "Satan assigned his imps to murder me, but I know a power that is greater than his. In the name of Jesus, I have the victory. When God says 'live', even five bullets can't take a life."

Explaining the facts surrounding the shooting in spiritual terms, I said: "It was a hit man from Hell."

"When God has His hand on you, nobody can kill you; I mean, nobody. The host of Heaven got me off my feet. Not many people, shot with a 9-millimeter semiautomatic weapon at close range live to tell the story."

That night I told the congregation about the revelation God had given me about the Holy Ghost.

"Friends, the Holy Ghost is not just for salvation—He even regenerates *skin*. I called Bishop and told him that I could see the wounds on my arm healing while I watched." And then there was the revelation about the power of prayer.

"The tube in my throat made it sore. It made talking difficult, so I prayed, 'God, I know that this tube is helping to save my life, but if it won't risk my health could You have them remove the tube? I would appreciate it.

"That same day the doctors came in and said, 'we're removing the tube.'

"Since that prayer had worked so well, I decided that I would try another. I asked if they could remove the tubes in my belly. Done. Then the tubes in my arm—and soon I was home."

I ended by pointing to the crowd in the balcony, the main floor, and the choir loft, saying: "I thank you, you, and you for praying."

I was so excited that I jumped out of the pulpit and started dancing, forgetting that I was still too weak.

As I took my seat, they began to sing *Joy Bells,* and the choir chimed in with harmony: *Joy bells keep ringing in my heart. Joy bells keep ringing in my heart. Joy bells, joy bells, joy bells keep ringing in my heart.*

Eventually, it quieted down and the pastor began to preach the sermon, *I Have Something to be Thankful for: How About You?* Bishop Ellis used Psalm 118, as his scripture text.

He preached with such fervor that for a little while I forgot my troubles. It was a pep rally for 1993, and the message gave us hope for a better year. I needed all the inspiration that I could get.

18

Exception to the Rules

Going to church was the beginning of reasserting my independence. I wanted to get back to my home as soon as possible. I hadn't lived with my parents since I left in 1974 to rent my first apartment. They were great hosts, but I needed my space.

The kids and I were devising a way for me to come home. They felt that they were old enough to handle my care with the aid of their Aunt Saun. It was this crew that had taken care of me in August when I had crushed my knees. They did a good job then, and knew they could do it again.

With an unhealed scar that replaced the twenty-six staples from my breasts to my pelvic bone, how was I going to negotiate the stairs to my bedroom? My oldest son, Aaron, decided to move my bed to the dining room; it was a good plan but turned out to be too drafty.

Aaron returned it to my bedroom and I scooted up the stairs on my rear. Once upstairs, I stayed put. The family supplied all that I needed.

Before everyone left in the morning, they had assignments. Adam, the youngest, was to cook my breakfast, since he was the last one to leave home. Saun, Angela, and Aaron divided the other chores. One of them got my water, fruit juice and whatever else I might need before they left.

So, by the first week in January I went home. Aaron had been the "head of the house" since his father left in March, 1992, and at 15 was doing his best to fill those shoes. He was already a little bossy—Angela and Adam hated when I left them home with him in charge. Now the shooting intensified his efforts. I watched the child in him disappear

75

and a man emerging, much too soon. To shift the adult responsibilities to Aaron saddened me. Not only that, I found it uncomfortable receiving orders from my children. I gave the orders; they responded. Temporarily out of commission, and Saun unprepared to handle an invalid and three teenagers, they stepped up and handled my care.

Saun was upset with me, too. One day she said "A man shot you five times, at close range, yet you don't act like it? You act all big and bad like nothing happened."

Her outburst surprised me. I wasn't acting. Years working as a probation officer taught me not to show my emotions in trouble; it could intensify the problem. So, I learned to react on the inside only.

She screamed. "Your behavior's not normal. I need to see you cry, sweat, and show fear like any other normal human being."

"I'll see what I can do about that Saun." I replied, sarcastically. Saun's son, Darrell Jr. (Dee Dee) and my Aaron were both attending the same high school. Aaron was on the basketball team. One day both boys were eating lunch in the cafeteria when a hostile team member hollered at Aaron: "I wish your mother had died."

My nephew, Dee Dee, leaped up from the table and began swinging at him. Aaron tried to break up the fight up, and in the end, the principal expelled all three.

Cass Technical High School had a zero tolerance policy about fighting, no matter how good the reason. In my condition, this new ordeal upset me. Mr. Cohen, the principal, scheduled the hearing for both boys. Darrell and I needed to appear, since we both were the custodial parents.

I called Mr. Cohen.

"This is Mrs. Thomason, and I don't know how I can attend this hearing. Anyway, my son Aaron was only trying to break up a fight. Why did you exclude him?"

"I'm sorry, Mrs. Thomason," he said, "but we have rules at this school or we would have anarchy. You wouldn't want your son to attend a school which tolerates violence."

I hung up and began to pray, asking God to intervene in the matter. The day before the hearing I talked one more time with Mr. Cohen. He didn't want me to attend the hearing. He thought it was too risky for my fragile health. He'd had time to research the matter and discovered the other student, Al, was the Spanish Department head's son, and had a history of getting into trouble. Aaron, an honor student, never violated the rules. Aaron even wrote a letter of apology for his role in the incident, which impressed Mr. Cohen.

He told me over the phone "Aaron Thomason is a student that we want to keep at Cass. I can't promise you that I'll be forgiving, but I'll see what I can do."

In the end, he gave them all a break. In time, Dee Dee and Aaron both graduated from Cass Tech, but the other student continued getting in trouble and later was expelled.

19

Move Over, Sherlock Holmes

While I was still on a medical leave of absence, my co-workers were busy looking for my enemy. The sleuths of the Michigan Department of Corrections jumped into action. They had to find the shooter before he tried again.

In August of 1986, juvenile delinquents murdered their probation officer while she was on duty. This trend had to stop. My co-workers posted the suspect's picture at their workstations. Maybe a client knew the shooter and was willing to cooperate.

At church, the prayer warriors stayed busy interceding for me. First, they prayed for my life; then for a speedy recovery, that God would find the perpetrator, and justice prevail. They lived by James 5:16b…"The effectual fervent prayer of a righteous man availeth much." These intercessors—some I knew, and many of whom I didn't—all were on a mission to find the shooter.

While they prayed and I recovered my health, a few strange events happened. Within the first 30 days of my sick leave, my employer lost my paycheck. Then I received a strange call from my supervisor, Grace Jackson.

"Hello."

"Hello Denise. This is your supervisor, Grace. How are you doing?" She asked.

"I am doing fine. Grace, my last paycheck never arrived. I will see everyone today because I am picking up my replacement. Will you be there?"

"You didn't get that last check? We mailed it some time ago. Oh well, this gives us a chance to see you."

"Good. Who is supervising my clients?"

"Don't worry about them. We split your caseload up among the other agents. How's the investigation going with the police?"

"I haven't heard anything since the one line-up I went to when released from the hospital back in December."

"Why don't you call the police and see if they have any new leads?" She suggested.

She sounded secretive, almost as if she knew something I didn't.

"I will," I said, and hung up.

I called Sgt. Parker. He wasn't available. I left a message for him to call me and continued with my plans for the day. I was still on sick leave, but with aggressive physical therapy I had regained my ability to drive.

Excited, I was going to the job to get my replacement check, and to see my co-workers. I hoped that seeing me would help them believe I was going to live and not die. Soon I would be back to work, helping to keep the Motor City safe again. I also needed to know if I could return to that building without fear. This was the litmus test. Was I healed enough to enter it?

I went to the administrative office to get the new check. Hugs, smiles, and greetings from well-wishers met me.

"Denise," cried Linda. "I'm so glad to see you. My church and I were praying for you."

"You look so good," said another friend.

"You don't look like a person just shot."

"Have they found the person who did this to you?"

It was good to see everyone and hear the genuine affection in his or her voice.

I left the administrative offices and continued to the Tether Unit. Before I had a chance to soak up all the love, I got summonsed by the supervisor of parole, Mr. Harden.

"Have you talked with Grace Jackson, your supervisor? Do you know what's happened?"

"Happened? I questioned.

He took me to his office, shut the door, and lowered his voice so no one could overhear our conversation.

"Parole officer Rufus Moore received a possible lead from his client, Arthur Wideman. Wideman said he knew the guy who shot 'that woman probation officer.' Moore had asked his name, and he'd said, 'Mark, or something like that. I don't know. I'll tell you on my next visit. The guy was bragging to my friends and I that he'd shot her.'"

"Then Moore told me that he thought that Wideman looked like the composite. He even told him: 'Man, you look a lot like the man in the composite.'"

"You are kidding, right?" I said in unbelief?

"No!" Said Mr. Harden as he continued. "That revelation made the client nervous. When Moore told him that your cubicle was just across the aisle from him, Wideman began to perspire. He looked as if he'd seen a ghost. His cool, calm, jive-talk changed. He fidgeted in his seat. Beads of perspiration appeared on his brow. The routine office visit transformed into a tense torture chamber for the client. His once cocky air of importance changed."

Mr. Harden went on: "Wideman said he had a friend who shot that woman, but he kept peering across the aisle. Moore said he seemed distracted as though at any minute you were going to appear in your office and recognize him as the shooter. He seemed glad when the interview was over, said his good-byes, and rushed out of the office."

"Wow, that's some story." It overpowered me. I wasn't prepared for it.

Harden was not through, "Moore said, Wideman's nervousness made him suspicious. Wideman has since failed to keep any further appointments."

"Mr. Harden, what do you want me to do with this information?'

"Denise, we passed this information on to my boss who told his boss Jerome Jones. We even called Sgt. Winston Parker, the police officer in charge, but he didn't follow up on this lead. A couple of weeks have gone by and the police still haven't taken action."

While we were talking, I realized that only the shooter and I knew some of the details Wideman had told the parole officer. Usually, when a client is guilty of committing a crime, he blames the act on a friend. I became more and more suspicious of Wideman.

"Mr. Harden, do you have the file?"

He reached in his drawer and produced it. I picked up the portfolio, opened it, and looked at the picture with horror. This was the man who stood over me with flaring nostrils and green mist rolling out of his head.

Suddenly, my beating heart sounded like thunder within me. My lungs were gasping for oxygen as though someone had siphoned the air from the room. What should I do? How could I safely get from the building to my car in the parking garage? Dark and shadowy, a perfect place for an ambush.

Mr. Harden looked concerned. "Denise, what's wrong?" He half-rose from his chair and leaned across his desk. "Shall I call for help?"

"No," I lied, trying as always not to let my emotions show in public. I held out the file to Mr. Harden saying, "This is the man. I'm positive."

When it was time to leave, I rushed through the garage in terror, hoping to get into my car and out of there without another attempt on my life. I was paranoid. The enemy—who had once been nameless and faceless, now had a face and body. I imagined him as being only a few steps away. He was not anonymous any more; he now was too close for comfort. He knew who I was, and I knew who he was.

From then on, the search for Mr. Wideman began, and my co-workers in the Department of Corrections were the heroes. Mr. Moore issued a warrant for violation of parole. He failed to report as stipulated in the parole agreement. The Absconder's Unit, assigned to arrest him, went to his house and left messages for him to report. Initially, he ignored them; but the officers' persistence frightened his family. The Absconders' Unit turned up the heat, and the last message left for him was to *report to his parole officer and he might receive leniency.*

It worked. On his arrival, Rufus Moore handcuffed him and turned him over to the Detroit Police Department.

First, I needed to identify the shooter. At a photo line up I identified him without a problem. Next, I identified him during a live line up. This one did not intimidate me like the last one did. I was not under heavy medication.

On March 1, 1993, nearly three months after the shooting, the 36th district judge, Danny Smart, arraigned him on the charges of Assault with Intent to Murder, Assault with Intent to Rob Armed, and being a Felon in Possession of a Firearm.

March 1 was also my first day back to work. What a red-letter day that was.

20

Bouncing Back

I returned to work with a hero's welcome. Everyone was so surprised to see me. Most thought I returned to work too soon. They didn't understand that God gave me a speedy recovery.

However, I still had some questions, even a theory, that this was not a random shooting. The man performed with too much precision. Why did this man see me as an enemy? He shot me too many times for the typical robber, what was his motive? Was he hired to murder me? I needed to solve this mystery. The police needed my help. I asked God to strengthen me quickly so I could find out what happened.

During my first day back to work, I spoke with many co-workers. They all had their theories surrounding the incident. Some said this would support the efforts of our union officials to sanction our wearing a gun seven days a week, twenty-four hours a day. Malcolm asked me to join the cause.

One co-worker, Mercury Smith, met me in the hall and shared his concern. He had shared the facts of my case with an FBI friend, who had told him to warn me to be careful.

"Tell that woman to be careful. This was not a random robbery. It sounds like a contract for hire. Someone wanted her dead."

This was the first person that echoed my suspicion.

That morning I requested a transfer from the Tether Unit because the unit was not secure enough to stop the would-be murderer from trying again. My staying at the same location not only placed *me* in danger, but everyone who worked with me. This worked. When I tried to get the transfer for my own protection, no one listened. But when risking the safety of others, my superiors listened.

One client already proved the flaw in our security. Mr. Malone walked past the receptionist desk to my office unnoticed. I didn't want to give him another opportunity. Permission granted. On March 2, 1993, I reported for duty to my old unit, the Northwest Probation District.

Work at my previous unit took some adjustment. The people there were like family. Most knew me since the beginning of my career. We shared intimate experiences together. However, it took time to adjust to the new me. I looked the same, but I wasn't. Foggy thoughts and slow, deliberate speech highlighted the *new* me. Nothing about the post-shooting me resembled the past. I hoped the familiarity would put me back together.

Some coworkers surprised me. Joseph said, "If you can't do the work, go home." I thought we were buddies. Carleton kept tabs on each piece of work assigned to me. He wanted me to get my equal portion of the workload. I wanted some compassion since I always did my work and sometimes a portion of theirs. I wanted some slack until I made a full recovery. Wouldn't you think that a little compassion was in order?

It was tough to act normal while wearing two knee braces. Then there was the problem with recurring bouts of diarrhea caused from having a shorter colon. The bullets damaged both of them, one patched up and the other resectioned. This made weekly interviews of my clients difficult, especially after lunch.

Once a week I conducted in person, one-on-one interviews with my clients. We called it report day. I was available all day, in fact, the same day each week. Clients arrived by appointments only. A report day consisted of my being available in the office to meet with clients in person, one-on-one. State law mandated my clients to report at least once a month. Each client filled out a written form documenting his or her whereabouts and changes in addresses, phone number, employment, schooling, and new arrest.

Bowel spasms kept me in the bathroom most of the time. My slowness caused the reception room to overcrowd. Tensions increased and friction broke out among the clients. Their agitation drained more strength from me.

I still had to take time off to go to physical therapy, so I tried taking my lunch hour and an hour of sick leave to allow me enough time for the medical care. My supervisor reduced my caseload and reduced the number of investigations. This upset some of my co-workers, which made work doubly hard for me.

On March 30, Gregory Malone called my office. He is the client who confronted me on December 8, 1992—the one who said that he was not going to prison. He called to discuss the probation hearing. He and his attorney went to court that day and he said the judge charged him with violating his probation. He was calling me to tell me the violation hearing would be in June. He didn't like my response.

"Sir, you should have pleaded guilty. You would have had a better chance for leniency or mercy from the court. My testimony will damage your case."

When we hung up, I heaved a sigh of relief. I thought, *well, at least I don't have to deal with that issue until June.*

The rest of that day was uneventful. At five o'clock that evening, I signed out and was officially off duty. I mentioned to a few people who were still at work that I was going to stop at the local supermarket to buy groceries, and then I was going home.

It may have taken all of 15 minutes to pick up those groceries. Then I pulled out of the store's parking lot, made a left-hand turn, and headed east on West McNichols.

I relaxed. *In five minutes you'll be home. It will be good to see the children and cook dinner. Then I'm going to soak my sore knees and put on my pajamas.*

From in front of the car a loud, thundering, boom disrupted my thoughts. The glass in my windshield shattered. I ducked, clutching the steering wheel. The peace I'd experienced went out the window.

I can't believe this. I've got to get out of here. I pressed down on the accelerator. *A moving target is hard to hit,* I thought.

Since most of the damage was on the passenger side of the windshield, I could see well enough to drive home.

I looked around me, but no one was walking on the sidewalks, and there was no object in the roadway. The crash made no sense, except for the possibility of a sniper. If that were true, I knew to keep going.

When I arrived home, I drove in and parked the car in the backyard.

The kids were watching television, and I poked my head in the room and said, "Kids, would you get the groceries out of the trunk?"

They came trooping out and I couldn't resist hugging them, saying "I'm so *glad* to be home. Oh, and by the way, don't worry, something hit the windshield on the way home."

So far, I had managed to hide my terror from the children, and wanted nothing more than to draw my house in around me. Terror kept me from calling the police, and I did not make a police report later. I just wanted to hide, at my home, and be safe.

The next day at work, we were short of supervisors. If I remember correctly, my manager, Carleton Foster, had just returned to work from his own life-threatening illness. He, too, struggled to regain his strength to handle our district. I needed to tell him what happened the night before. He was the only official superior available to write the critical incident report.

He listened, but said only, "Hmm."

There was no more said. I didn't push the issue since, technically, it happened in the gray area of the law. On duty or not? This was the same question that was asked, by my superiors, on the day of the shooting. According to Michigan law, probation officers are still on duty up to one hour after leaving work. I was within that time frame. No one liked gray area issues, especially then.

On March 31, when a mobile unit came and replaced my wind-shield, at my expense, I felt abandoned by my employer. Not only that, I was becoming paranoid. Did one of my own coworkers have me set up? Only a few people knew I went shopping.

I thought to myself, *Look, Denise, you need to be careful with your mouth. You need to keep your private life quiet. Tell it only on a need to know basis. Who can you trust?*

It wasn't just this incident alone that upset me, but the lack of concern for my safety. No one ever debriefed me. Yet, I saw inaccurate memos about the incident portrayed as factual. No one asked me for the truth. Many people told me later that they thought my ex-husband shot me. Otherwise, they thought I was just in denial.

After I calmed down about what was clearly a second shooting, I called my friend, Yolanda Searls, who was a supervisor in Court Support.

"Yolanda, could you secure Gregory Malone's warrant file and send it to me? I have a June hearing for violation of his probation. Malone tried to bribe me earlier, and I want to review my notes to see what else I documented in the file. His wife called me and told me that he broke his house arrest monitoring computer. This equipment effectively recorded his whereabouts in his house, if not disabled.

Before each shooting, Malone and I had hostile conversations. I began wondering if there might be a connection.

After a few days, I received a call from Yolanda.

"Denise, I can't find that file on Malone. I talked with Donald Fountain, my boss and he told me, 'If you find the file make a copy and hide it.' I think he feels there's a possibility of an inside job."

Nothing happened for a month, so I called Yolanda again.

"I'm sorry, Denise," she said. "I've had the record room attendant hunting for the file, but he can't find it. I'm thinking that this file is long gone and I don't think it will ever surface."

I was becoming more and more fearful. In almost 19 years I never had a warrant file lost. The contents always were available to me for a violation hearing. Why now, at the height of my vulnerability, was this happening?

My memory was foggy and this client was hostile and shrewd, so I needed all the help that I could get. Everything about my job changed and so had the rules of engagement, making me feel like a stranger.

My administration seemed annoyed that I had lived. I had complicated circumstances and it didn't fit into the daily routine of the corrections department. It would have been easier for them if I died. Paying my estate and closing my file was simple and final; then they could replace me. At times I wished it happened just like that. Life was just too much to handle.

21

Crumbling Masks

Working as a probation officer, I needed to feel invincible. That belief gave me the guts to go where no one in his right mind should. Being a tethering agent was even worse; it was a very dangerous occupation. I tried to transfer without success; so, for protection, I learned to use a gun.

As the Bible tells us, fear is a tormentor. (I John 4:18) It's the bully on the playground who taunts his prey by calling him a sissy. Then when the "sissy" turns and faces his enemy, striking an unsuspecting blow, the bully goes home.

Just so I could deal with danger, I learned to use a gun.

At first that was a powerful feeling. I stalked around knowing I could take on the bad guys. However, a few close calls proved the gun was not always accessible.

Minimally, I carried two awkward boxes into homes when installing tethering equipment: a bulky toolbox, and a large suitcase-looking box with the computer and accessories for house arrest. When I unzipped my belly bag holster to get my gun, it would be too late.

So I had to use another weapon. I found a Scripture in 2 Timothy 1:7: *For God hath not given us the spirit of fear; but of power, and of love, and of a sound mind.*

Fear was not of God; therefore, whenever afraid, I repeated it over and over in prayer.

Another Scripture that helped in the time of need was Psalm 91:1: *He that dwelleth in the secret place of the most High shall abide under the shadow of the Almighty.*

These scriptures, and many others, are powerful words to fight fearful thoughts.

I allowed fear to control my life. I decided important issues based on it. I created excuses to hide behind it. I imagined negative outcomes, and hesitated to perform. So, to control fear, I had to use 2 Corinthians 10:4-5 often. It states:

For the weapons of our warfare are not carnal, but mighty through God to the pulling down of strong holds; Casting down imaginations, and every high thing that exalteth itself against the knowledge of God, and bringing into captivity every thought to the obedience of Christ....

Fear also caused me to lose self-respect and accept mistreatment from my employer.

To avoid loneliness, I accepted disrespectful and inappropriate behavior from coworkers, too. It saddens me when I look back at the humiliation I allowed myself to endure. In all fairness to me, I did the best that I could at the time.

The fear habit began during childhood. I felt powerless to confront my fears, so I chose alternative ways to kill the red light that signaled danger.

In short, I learned to overachieve, to keep too busy to feel fear, to overeat, and to help others. These coping skills helped to quiet my fearful thoughts.

Unfortunately, these ways of coping didn't eliminate the issues; I just learned to hide them. After a while, I buried fear so far inside me that I forgot about what bothered me. I disconnected the warning signals. When danger came I ignored it. I also failed to respond to the "flight or fight" instinct.

I dated bad boys. I thought their inappropriate behavior didn't frighten me. Don't brave people respond that way? Wasn't I brave dating them? The answer is no! I felt an uneasiness deep down inside. I didn't understand it, so I continued dating dangerous men, mistaking fear for love. God tried to warn me. I couldn't decipher the muffled message.

Then I picked one of the most dangerous jobs for my vocation. I couldn't understand why people would stare at me when I discussed my career.

"Isn't that *dangerous?*" Was the question that usually followed.

"Well, yes," I'd reply, feeling a certain smugness in my skill to work the job.

"Doesn't that frighten you?"

"No," I'd reply. *What a silly question, I thought. Why would danger make me afraid? I was, after all, invincible.*

22

Born Again Boss

Then my friend, Countessa Cortland, became my supervisor. She, too, was a born-again Christian and helpful. Her words encouraged me. She knew the language I spoke, and, in my weariness, she gave me good spiritual encouragement.

She'd say, "Don't let the devil defeat you."

On report days, my colon problems created a back up of clients in the reception area. This created impatient people.

On some days, to avoid working overtime, I interviewed my clients in groups of four or more. Each client wanted my individual attention, and they didn't like it. My manager assigned me eighty new clients in a ninety-day period; it created a problem. Humanly speaking, when not injured that was a difficult task.

My knees created a problem, since without notice, one or both knees could lock up. If that happened, I had to have another officer bring my clients back to my office, or I had to move to an office closer to the door.

I had a few confrontations with my co-workers. Jeremy, a long-time acquaintance, had the loudest mouth. He'd been sick with out-of-control sugar diabetes. If anyone should understand disability, I felt he would be the one. He didn't. I was also a good customer of his wife, who was a caterer. He'd forgotten that I had bought a few cakes from his wife, and he said: "If you can't pull your weight, then you should go home."

It surprised and hurt me to hear this from someone I called my friend, so I kept trying harder to stay afloat.

However, Countessa Cortland stayed in my ear, saying softly: *You can do all things through Christ who strengthens you.*

God used her as my angel on-the-job.

Next, I needed to renew my carrying concealed weapons permit (CCW). It expired during my recovery. Each job-related injury interfered with my yearly gun training (re-certification). The administration gave me one more appointment to re-certify. I had to pass it or give up the permit until I was well enough to complete the training.

Carleton Foster said, "Denise, sympathy about the shooting is running out. Management is going to remove your permit if you miss this re-certification."

In May of 1993, the regional administrator, Keith Smith, annulled my permit. I appealed to his boss, the administrator of operations, Duncan Long. I wrote a letter asking permission to carry my gun until after the trial. I explained to him that I needed to protect the prosecution's key witness, me.

"*Permission denied!*" His letter said. Instead he sent me a canister of pepper spray.

"Enclosed is a can of pepper spray. Use this for your protection until you become strong enough for gun training."

Imagine. *Pepper spray.*

Rage engulfed me. Didn't he realize that I was the victim of a murder plot? Instead, he wanted me to fend off bullets with pepper spray.

I felt abandoned, expendable. First my coworkers failed me, and now the administration. No mercy or grace expressed on this job. No one understood my predicament. My supervisor tried to explain their position; I couldn't hear her either. She empathized, but did not compromise.

However, the department did give me administrative leave to attend the trial, which gave me time off with pay. I appreciated that.

23

Dressed Up but Messed Up

I thought Mortimer was the reason my life was at a standstill. Now that he was gone, I could have the life that I deserved. I thought, my life was going to soar once getting a divorce. Oh, how shortsighted and selfish I was.

I began my new life by getting more involved in church. A small-groups ministry began at church, designed to keep people from getting lost in a big church. Parishioners could feel plugged into the larger church through their smaller groups. It was innovative and exciting to me. It was simply called, "Birth Months" ministry. It included each church member; each automatically belonged. This created twelve groups in which members could:

1. Volunteer once a year as a group to help during their birth month in Children's Church

2. Give everyone a special group to belong to with a common interest

3. When a church member was in need, the group members met that need.

I ate that up. It met my needs not only for a social life, but offered me another opportunity to serve, both of which I needed. Another ministry trying to get off the ground was the single's group. I was already a minister and Children's Church director. I seized the new opportunity to volunteer my service. I helped to set that up, was part of the board of directors, and an instructor. All of these projects, three children, and my job helped to fill the void of Mortimer's departure.

I wanted to prove to him that one less monkey wasn't going to stop my show. Life would go on. I was also on the lookout for a new love interest. New adrenaline pumped through my veins. God gave me a second chance to find happiness. The new group involvement eased my loneliness.

I still had a job, my children, and other church responsibilities. Even so, Mortimer's leaving me for another woman, younger than me, made me want to prove that I still was young enough to compete. As a bail-out, in case no one came to claim me, I had my projects. Church became a good place to hide. Maybe I'd find a good, saved churchgoer and live happily ever after.

This plan kept eroding, subtly at first. The drive to my new work site changed from a six-minute drive into a 26-mile round-trip journey through bumper-to-bumper traffic. Then there was the injury to my knees, followed by the shooting. Still, I could handle it. I'd rise above all the drama and land right on solid ground like I always did.

After eighty-two days of grueling rehabilitation I was back to work, and everything was back to normal—so I thought.

I didn't realize I was all dressed up, but messed up. No amount of busyness was going to fix the broken pieces inside. God was at work in me, and it was only a matter of time before I would realize it.

In April 1993, Barry Stone, a church member whose birth month was February (the same as mine) was in a near-fatal car accident. Our group rallied around Barry. I gathered all the necessary information and called to see what he needed.

He lived-in an apartment by himself, was barely eating, and in pain. Knowing he needed me, I went home, cooked food, and took it to him. I didn't feel safe in the area surrounding his apartment building. Inside, the long dark, dingy corridors added to my fear. After the shooting, places like that made me especially uneasy.

Barry met me at the door because there was no buzzer to let me in. He was a frail-looking man with about six dirty teeth. He looked like a magpie dipped in dark chocolate, and was about half a head shorter than I. He slowly maneuvered himself to the door on two crutches.

In the accident, he broke his thighbone, and a rod was holding the pieces together. I was uneasy about entering his apartment alone, but duty called, so I sucked it up and helped the brother. When it was my turn to suffer, I remembered how helpless I had felt.

Over and again I repeated these visits of mercy, until he began depending on me. He shooed away all the other helpers so as to depend on me. It was a little taxing, but it was also flattering. After a while, he made his intents known that he liked me and I began acting like a blushing schoolgirl.

Before the accident, I would have thought he'd lost his mind, trying to get fresh with me. But now I was thankful for any attention. My mind was not seeing clearly and I thought he was my knight in shining armor. A man who put his teeth on lay-away was my new suitor. What a pair—both of us were too messed up to help each other. It was a case of the blind leading the blind.

We were both still going to physical therapy and taking heavy-duty pain pills. I was his chauffeur and confidant. Together we fought loneliness and the devil. I liked his company because he talked about the Bible and treated me as though I were special. He was one of the few people who knew how it felt to almost die unexpectedly.

I gave him my number at work and my home number so he could call day and night if he needed anything…and he did just that. At my own invitation he held on to me and wasn't letting go.

On the other hand, I was low on energy; so I didn't have a whole lot to give out. I could cry and tell him my fears. He would pray and send me back out with a pep talk.

"You can do all things through Christ who strengthens you."

It was a difficult time to be needy.

The bumps in the road of my life became more like car-eating chuckholes. You know the kind—the ones that swallow up your car, break your tie-rods and collapse both wheels, making steering impossible. My life was out of control just like that jalopy. Oh, if only I realized it.

Playing make-believe became harder and harder to play each day. It took me longer to talk, walk and to think. That extra mile became too much. I began using vacation hours to cover my tardiness.

Then, too, I couldn't go anywhere without someone recognizing me. They remembered me either from the newspaper or from the telecasts. I kept a low profile. I didn't want any recognition. I had an enemy out there somewhere and I didn't want him to sneak up on me. My off-duty time was mine and I wanted to go back to being unknown.

24

Truth on Trial

When I looked at the picture of the parolee in the parole file, I jeopardized the case being thrown out. Was it legal for me to see it, or not? Did it prejudice my objectivity or fairness?

The defense attorney challenged the issue. He sought a special Walker Hearing before the trial. The judge heard the petition and adjudicated my identification of the shooter as permissible evidence.

Fortunately, I gave a description of the perpetrator *before* I saw the parole file. My description of height was accurate and the weight was only five pounds off. The defense attorney's cross-examination did not shake my testimony. My memory etched the shooter's description in the archives. I was certain that man in the picture was the same person in court.

Before going to court, I prayed. "God give me strength to endure the hearing."

The judge ruled my testimony as believable. In fact, the picture I saw in the parole file was different from the one I saw in the picture line-up.

On Monday June 7, 1993 at 9:23 a.m., the deputy sheriff said: "All rise. The Honorable Roberto Turner presiding for The Superior Court of Detroit, Michigan, in the county of Aspen."

I took the beginning trial information from the transcript. The judge sequestered me, from the trial. No one wanted me, the key eyewitness, to hear other testimony before giving mine.

The Clerk said, "This is file No. 93-02443, People versus Arthur Wideman. The charges are: Assault with Intent to Murder, Assault with Intent to Rob Armed, and Possession of a Firearm in the Commission or Attempt to Commit Felony."

The judge said, "Good morning, ladies and gentlemen of the jury."

"Good morning, your Honor," said the jury.

"I'd like to thank you for coming down, accepting the Court's invitation to serve as jurors. The case that some of you will hear will not take up a lot of your time. We should be able to finish this case before Wednesday, most likely tomorrow. So if any of you have anything important to do next week or the end of this week, you don't have to make excuses to get out of serving because this is not going to be a long trial."

A few jurors nodded their heads in affirmation.

"Let me introduce you to the attorneys who will try this case. First, let me introduce you to the assistant prosecutor, Esther Wickham."

Ms. Wickham addressed the jurors by saying "Good morning, ladies and gentlemen."

The members of the prospective jury replied, "Good morning."

"My name is Esther Wickham and I'm the assistant prosecutor. I work for Aspen County, and this is Sergeant Parker, who investigated this case. Thank you."

Judge Turner continued. "And representing Mr. Wideman is attorney Joseph Bussy."

Mr. Bussy turned to address the jurors, saying "Good morning, everybody."

A harmony of voices said, "Good morning."

"My name is Joseph Bussy. My office is here in Detroit, and I represent Arthur Wideman. He's seated right in front of me."

Judge Turner turned his attention back to the jurors' box once all the introductions and greetings ended.

"Do any of you ladies and gentlemen know Ms. Wickham, Mr. Bussy or Mr. Arthur Wideman, the defendant in this case? Any of you know any of these people?"

"No," they all replied.

The courtroom drama began to unfold. It was like a boxing match. In one corner was the prosecuting attorney, who represented the violation of my rights. In the other corner was the defense attorney, Mr. Bussy, who was representing the defendant, Arthur Wideman. Then the referee, the Honorable Roberto Turner, and to weigh the matter, the jury. Everyone took his or her place; then the attorneys came out fighting.

The prosecutor began first. A young, confident, blonde prepared and convinced she would persuade the jury of Mr. Wideman's guilt. The intensity of her opening argument set the climate. She described a graphic picture of the crime scene and invoked compassion toward me. Each word counted toward the expected victory.

Ms. Wickman said, "Now the crime of Assault with Intent to Murder requires, simply, that Mr. Wideman tried to physically injure Denise Thomason. That when he was committing this assault, he had the ability to do some harm. And that in his mind, when he was committing the assault, he intended to kill her."

My brother Rex told me later that some jurors squirmed in their seats at the mention of the word kill. Others showed their displeasure with frowns or a furrowed forehead. Some seemed unaffected by the words and sat attentively waiting for what was next.

"Now, an intent to kill can be determined in several ways. Sometimes people say, 'I'm trying to kill you.' More often you have to discover their intent by what they are *doing*. Ladies and gentlemen, when you shoot somebody five times in the stomach, you intend to kill them."

Ms. Wickham continued: "The prosecution charged Mr. Wideman with a second crime, Assault with Intent to Rob while Armed. This is like an attempted armed robbery, because he didn't get anything. An Armed Robbery requires that he took some money or some property. An Assault with Intent to Rob while Armed requires, first off, again, like the first one, that he assaulted her.

"And third, that when he assaulted her, he intended to rob her, and that means to take some property. We know that because he pulled a weapon originally and he said, 'Give it to me,' or 'Give it up,' or something of that sort. You will hear the details from Ms. Thomason.

"Finally, he is charged with an add-on charge of Possessing a Firearm While Committing a Felony. If you find he committed either of the felonies—the Assault with Intent to Murder, or Assault with Intent to Rob—if he had a gun when he did it, that's the third charge."

Next up was the defense attorney, Mr. Bussy.

Mr. Bussy: "Good morning, everybody."

The Jury: "Good morning."

Mr. Bussy: "As you heard, this case involves the senseless shooting of a probation officer, Denise Thomason. And for that, I think we are all sorry, you know. This is a tough city sometimes, and you hear about these senseless crimes every day. But we will also hear another case. About an over-zealous parole officer who is trying to railroad Mr. Wideman here in 1993 in America.

"Mr. Wideman is on parole for Attempted Larceny over a Hundred Dollars. Mr. Wideman reported to Rufus Moore, both before and after the shooting. After the shooting, Mr. Wideman went into the office, as you heard the prosecutor say, and noticed the composite sketch on the wall. It was up in the parole officer's office because that's his co-worker. She works a couple desks over. People are in and out. I don't know whether Denise Thomason ever saw Mr. Wideman while he was reporting for parole, but she could have. I don't know.

"But in any event, Mr. Wideman was talking to the parole officer about the shooting and looking at the composite, and the parole officer says, 'Hey, you look like this guy', which is not true. You can look at the composite and see the thick mustache and hood and perhaps a goatee. I can't tell. But I don't think it looks anything like Mr. Wideman.

"But in any event, they had a conversation about the shooting because the picture was on the wall there.

"Then two months later, after Denise Thomason finally recovered and got out of the hospital, she went in to pick up her check. And it [was] then the parole officer said, 'Hey, I have a picture for you. We were talking about your shooting and look, here he is, or here the picture is. Look at that picture.' It was a single photograph—there was no attorney present. She looked at that photograph and said, 'That's the man that shot me.'

"Well, I believe the police tried to make her claim true by creating a second photo line up with the same picture. The second line up an attorney was present. And, of course, she picked out the same photograph of the man she saw in the parole file.

"Then they did a live line-up. Of course, she picked out Mr. Wideman because that's the photograph she saw initially.

"Now, I want to back up. I understand Denise Thomason that she wants to get the person that did this crime. I would like to get him too. I just know it's not Mr. Wideman. This identification two months after the fact just doesn't make any sense to me. It's too good to be true. It's too much of a coincidence.

"Rufus Moore arrested Mr. Wideman when he reported February 9th voluntarily to his parole officer. He walked into the office, and by that time they'd got the case moving along and they said, 'You're the man.' And that's when he was arrested on a voluntary report to his parole officer. He wasn't arrested at home, or he wasn't arrested out on the street with a 9mm. He was arrested two months later after a two-month gap in the identification. There's no smoking gun, or anything. But, this is just too much of a coincidence for me.

"And I want you to look, too, at the identification aspect of the event itself, the shooting. The shooting happened at night, a hooded suspect. There were two or three or four perpetrators [so] that identity in and of itself is wrong. But then when you couple that with two months later looking at a photograph and then trying to legitimize that with a photo line-up and a live line-up, it just doesn't make sense to me. Mr. Wideman never ran. He reported after the shooting to his parole officer. There's just too much doubt here on this case.

"I would like to get the perpetrator of this crime, too, but I don't want to push too hard and get the wrong fellow: Mr. Wideman. So, please find him not guilty."

Mr. Bussy was a good rival. He knew how to present the law as both fact and speculation. It wasn't going to be an easy win. At the end of round one, no one had the advantage.

I testified first, the prosecutor's key eyewitness. My family supported me. Their presence in court gave me courage.

At eleven o'clock, the court clerk swore me in. I testified for an hour; this included examination by the prosecutor and the defense. The whole ordeal made me tired, telling the same story over and over again. I had to remember the painful details. I just wanted this nightmare to end.

My knees ached and my colons threatened a diarrhea episode. I prayed, "God please don't let my colons act up now." He honored that prayer; during my testimony I did not have to stop testifying to use the toilet. I managed to testify to the truth to the best of my ability.

At last, Judge Turner said, "Ms. Thomason, you may step down."

Before stepping down, I adjusted both of my support braces on my kneecaps, and hobbled to a seat next to my family and friends. It was over.

Contrary to expectations, it turned out to be a three-day trial. The prosecutor presented her case first and rested to hear the defense attorney's convincing argument that this man was innocent. In a surprising move, he offered no case.

He petitioned the judge to give a directed verdict for acquittal. He felt the prosecutor failed to prove his client guilty beyond a shadow of a doubt. Judge Turner, satisfied with the evidence presented by the prosecution, denied his request.

Mr. Bussy was so convinced that his strategy for no defense was correct that he rested his case without presenting one shred of evidence.

Mr. Wideman did not want to testify on his own behalf. Both sides made the closing remarks.

Judge Turner, by law, gave the jury instructions before they could deliberate the facts.

He said, "The judge is neutral. He acts as a referee and makes sure everything moves along smoothly. The jury is the trier of fact. Do not let your feeling affect the final decision. Any feelings of sympathy, bias or prejudice are not suitable for deliberation. You must be objective always; decide based on the evidence only."

Do not use Arthur Wideman's lack of testimony against him, the judge explained, explaining the defendant's right not to do so.

"The law does not need his testimony. His not testifying is not a sign of guilt and doesn't hold it against him. The burden of proof is on the prosecutor. Was there enough evidence presented to show guilt? The standard of proof is "beyond a reasonable doubt." All twelve of you must agree before you can present an acceptable verdict."

He further charged that they must decide if the testimonies of the witnesses were believable. He distinguished between a fact and an opinion. Judge Turner retired the jury, to the jury room, when he completed his instructions.

Judge Turner said: "You must pick a spokesperson among you who will be the foreman. That person will speak for the twelve."

They deliberated awhile, and then broke for lunch. After lunch they deliberated again. It was late and the jury had no decision. The judge brought them out to see if they were having trouble or needed another day.

The foreman said, "Your Honor, we're having trouble agreeing."

"Do you need more time?" Asked Judge Turner. "You tell me what you need to complete the job."

"I don't know if more time would help, sir," said the foreman.

My heart started racing—*not another trial. I just can't go through cross-examination again*, I thought.

Judge Turner said, "The jury did not reach a verdict? Another day will not help? Does everyone agree with his assessment?"

Juror number two spoke up, even though she was not the foreman.

"We can't be definite on that because at our last count there was an improvement."

Judge Turner asked, "Do you want to come back or go back now?"

Juror number two, "I'm tired today."

The frustrated judge, asked, "Well, then you tell me what to do?"

Juror number two, "Well, I just reminded our foreman that with our last count, there was an improvement. The count did change, and I think that is significant.

Judge Turner decided, "I will do whatever you ladies and gentlemen tell me to do. So if you want to stop and come back tomorrow, or...."

Juror number ten, the foreman, finally spoke up and said, "Everybody agrees—we'll start early tomorrow morning."

Heads nodded and the judge let them go home.

Judge Turner cautioned, "Don't talk about this, don't call one another, and don't discuss the case at all until you are in the jury room tomorrow morning at nine o'clock. Thank you. See you in the morning."

I couldn't believe that we almost had a mistrial. I went home discouraged, I decided to contact my prayer warriors. Aspen County was a county where juries favored defendants, and I could see I needed supernatural help.

Throwing myself on the mercy of my Heavenly Father, I prayed: "Lord, your Word says the truth will make me free. You stand for truth. I need You now to let the truth stand and not a lie."

25

The Prayer Closet

It worried me when it appeared the trial was going to end in a hung jury. God couldn't allow that to happen to me. Surely it was time for a turn-around.

When the children fell asleep, I put on my pajamas and prayed. As usual, I talked to God about the day's events, and in the middle of the chitchat I heard a small still voice say. *"Let me show you how to pray."*

I was listening.

"Turn to Proverbs 21:1-3."

I had nothing to lose, so I obeyed.

It read, *The king's heart is in the hand of the LORD, as the rivers of water: he turneth it whithersoever he will. Every way of a man is right in his own eyes: but the LORD pondereth the hearts. To do justice and judgment is more acceptable to the LORD than sacrifice.*

God's voice continued, *"Now, Denise, you need to pray the Word back to Me. Each juror represents the king. Each holds the power of decision-making in their vote. You want Me to meet them at their respective homes and review the facts of the case. You are a professional who has made a career remembering detail. Pray that they understand, that what you did the night of the shooting was normal. Remembering facial features, height, and weight and other distinguishing features is a must for your profession. You pray that, and I will do the rest. I am Truth, and the truth will prevail."*

My soul was alive with excitement. The Lord spoke to me. God Almighty took time-out to tell this fragile child how to use His Word in prayer. If only my knees had cooperated, I would have leaped up and danced for joy.

Instead, I prayed as directed, and added, "Please, God, don't let the jurors rest until they have reexamined the facts. While they sleep, let them hear the case in their dreams. I want them to believe my testimony. God, I have trusted in You most of my life, and I can't afford a defeat now."

There was no question that I believed that God was my Father and Jesus was His Son. I always believed that even when no one else was listening, that I had an audience in Heaven. This jury trial was no different. Praying gave me courage to face difficulties. It must work. When I was lying on the ground, bleeding, I prayed. Not only did help come, but God spared my life.

I still had one question unanswered, why didn't God stop the bullets after I called on the name of Jesus?

That question was an area of conflict that I had not resolved with God. I took one issue at a time. It was important for me to let Him show His power on the verdict. We could deal with the rest later.

26

Crime Doesn't Pay

The next morning was Wednesday, June 9, 1993. The court resumed at nine o'clock. All the jurors reported for duty. After the court clerk was sure that all were present, the deliberation continued. Two hours later they came to a verdict.

The court clerk addressed the jurors saying: "Members of the jury, have you agreed on a verdict and if so, who shall speak for you?"

Juror number ten stood and said, "I will."

The clerk continued: "How do you find for the defendant to count one?"

"Guilty of Assault with Intent to Murder"

"How do you find for the defendant to count two?"

"Count two, guilty of Assault with Intent to Rob Armed."

"How do you find for the defendant to count three?"

"Guilty of Possession of a Firearm while in Commission of a Felony."

The clerk had the whole jury panel stand and raise their right hands, showing that they were in one accord about the verdict. Then they polled them individually to affirm the same.

Judge Turner turned to the jury panel and said, "Ladies and gentlemen, we would like to thank you for your service. It's obvious you considered all the evidence and you gave every bit of evidence your consent before reaching a verdict in this case. The verdict matched the evidence.

"Now let me tell you, I have heard many witnesses testify since I've been on the bench and practicing law. When they tried to describe [their assailants], they were way off in the height or way off in the weight. But I never, ever heard a witness's description as perfect as the one Mrs. Thomason gave, only five pounds off on the weight. They don't do that well at Cedar Point. She was perfect. She gave every possible detail, without contradiction. And just think of all the hardships that she went through. She still kept the presence of mind to say, 'I'm going to make sure that this doesn't happen to anybody else because I'm going to remember this person.' You couldn't ask for anything other than [what] she gave you."

The judge went on and praised them for a good job. The judge set sentencing for nine o'clock, June 22nd.

I was glad, but did not feel the elation I thought I'd have. Before the trial God said, "Testify to the truth as you know it. The truth will surprise you.

I heard nothing different at the trial. I chose to let go of my job-related theory. But the facts still pointed to a murder contract. Thinking like that did me no good. I purposed, in my heart, that I was a victim of chance, in the wrong place at the wrong time.

27

Battered by the Storms

The trial was over. The stress of it drained my emotions. Now, I could put that behind me and begin to live again. Unfortunately, the trial was not my only obstacle. There were deadlines to meet at work. Then, too, I was also making other court appearances.

Mortimer petitioned the Friend of the Court for a decrease in child support. So I had to appear in court for that. He paid $136 a week for three kids, but after the hearing, because he wasn't working, it went down to $56 a week.

I had other court appearances for violation of probation for my clients. One judge was so mad when I arrived, she asked, "Where does the Probation Department get off changing my orders? I want my order followed just as I requested. Do you understand?"

Hmmm, I thought. *So, why is she yelling at me? What did I do? I am doing the best I can to follow her instructions. Is there no end to this emotional hammering? No matter what I do, I still come out on the short end of the stick. Well, hang in their, girl, you have three children to look after. They're counting on you to provide. We'll make it no matter what.*

My absence from work put me behind in meeting deadlines, and I was going slower and slower. However, I was getting some comfort from my supervisor, Countessa Cortland, who kept telling me: "You can do it. It won't always be this hard."

As a Christian, she knew what I needed to hear for encouragement.

Two days after the verdict, on June 11, 1993, I was sitting at my desk when the telephone rang. It was the receptionist, Amber.

"I have a man on the line, looking for the shot probation officer. Do you want to take the call?"

"Who is he? Why does he want to talk with me?" I asked.

"I don't know. I hesitated to put the call through, you decide."

Curious, I said: "Sure, let me talk with him."

"Ma'am, Ma'am, are you okay?" asked a male voice.

"Who is this?" I asked.

"I heard you were shot and I just wanted to know if it was true."

"Why do you want to know?"

"I was talking with a friend who said that he had shot his probation officer. I thought he was lying. I didn't know your name. He just told that his probation officer was a female."

Was this was a crank call?

He said: "I'm a born-again believer, and I couldn't rest 'until I found out if you're alright."

"Sir, I must know your name. I can't tell you anything until I know who you are." My breathing became labored.

"Ma'am, if I tell you that, he will kill me. I have some business partners that are ruthless. To protect myself I can't reveal my name."

I asked: "Who's the man who said he shot me?"

He hesitated. "Can you trace this call?"

"No," I said.

"His initials are 'GM. 'Do they match any client?"

"Gregory Malone?"

"Yes, if he knew that I was talking to you, he'd have me killed."

This was the second person in less than six months who had the same fear. In November, his wife was afraid, too. Now, that part of his story I believed. I lived with the scars and the pain inflicted by Gregory Malone.

He asked: "When did this happen?"

"In December."

"He asked to borrow my gun then. I told him no. If he did anything illegal, the police would come looking for me. Did you know that he bribed a judge?" The man asked.

"No."

"He went to court for violation of probation, and the judge threw out the warrant and the order for the tether. He lessened the probation sentence to six months coupled with drug screening. He only has six months to stay clean. I'll help find the man he hired to shoot you."

I hesitated, then said, "Sir, that won't be necessary. Two days ago, the jury found that man guilty."

"What does the guy look like?"

I described the man, and the caller said: "Well, it doesn't sound like anyone I know. I'm going to keep my ear to the ground, anyway. I want to get to the bottom of this."

Didn't God say "*Testify to what you know. The truth will surprise you.*"

Was this the missing piece I'd been looking for? This new information paralyzed my thoughts, leaving me numb. Stunned, I walked into Countessa's office in tears. She ended her phone call so she could address my concerns.

"What's wrong?" She asked.

I told her the story. She looked as startled as I felt. She processed the information quickly and started barking out orders.

"First, we have to prove his believability. Call the Denver County Court Clerk to see if any such sentencing occurred."

I called and confirmed it. The information this man gave us was correct down to the re-establishing an open probation case. Standard protocol after a hearing put me back into danger. My name as supervising probation officer put him back on my caseload. Since my employer felt the shooting was a random one, they took no measures to keep me safe.

No, there was no way I was going to supervise this man again.

Mrs. Cortland tried to assure me she would get the matter resolved to my favor. I didn't believe her. I began trembling, weak with terror.

Fortunately, I requested a few days vacation to speak at the annual church council, and go to court about child support payments. This gave me a chance to get a break from the drama.

28

Justice Prevails

It was June 22, 1993, at 9:49 in the morning, and time to see what justice the shooter would receive for shooting me.

The clerk opened by saying: "The defendant had a jury trial, and on June 9, 1993, they found him guilty as charged on all three counts. Also, on June 9, the defendant pleaded guilty to being a Habitual 4 Offender. Defendant is in court today, your Honor, for sentencing."

Before sentencing, the defendant had an opportunity to speak on his behalf. In Michigan, the victim also has an opportunity to give his or her statement—I elected to exercise my choice to speak. I spoke first.

I stood at the podium trying to steady my shaking voice and said: "On December 8th, Mr. Wideman wanted to take my natural life. He should give his as an exchange. These wounds are permanent. I must continuously attend physical therapy just to have an image of normalcy. My family, friends and anyone that knows me will carry the memory of this shooting. He doesn't deserve freedom."

"You can't get rid of my physical scars, but I believe the State of Michigan has a duty to then make sure he does not do this to any—any other person. It is the most violent act that a human being can experience. And by the grace of God I stand here, seeking justice. When I look at my arm, I remember. When I stand on my leg, I remember. When I use the bathroom, I remember. So I want to make sure that it is on record, Court of Appeals, that I want him confined for his natural life. Thank you, Your Honor."

Judge Roberto Turner said, "The Court remembers the facts in this case. Mr. Wideman shot her five times. He tried six but the cartridge ejected and didn't fire. And the intent in this case was to take her life. There should be no difference between a person who kills and a person who does everything possible to kill. The victim survived and did not die because of Divine intervention. And I know—I hope the Appeals Court doesn't accuse me of getting religious—but it's either luck or Divine intervention. Whatever they want to call it, that saved the complainant's life. It had nothing to do with the defendant. But the intent was the same, and the intent was there.

"The Court noticed, if this woman died, who could testify against him? No other person could identify the defendant as the shooter. He would still be out there.

"And the court heard him make a threat to the complainant after the jury verdict. He said, 'I'm going to get you.' I heard that.

Mr. Wideman interrupted and said: "I didn't say I was going to get you. I said, I ain't going to forget you."

Judge Turner continued: "Whatever it was, it was something to that effect. I construed it as a threat.

"And the testimony in this case was that he shot her while she was lying prostrate, I mean down, poor and helpless, and the gentlemen continued to fire.

"I had a chance to review all the facts in this case and I remember the testimony: how this woman was lying there and he continued to pump bullets into her. I know her injuries. He showed a lack of remorse and threatened her after the jury verdict. The Court must impose the severest penalty.

"So, for the first count of Assault with Intent to Commit Murder, the court is going to impose a sentence of not less than fifty (50) years. The maximum I will make one hundred (100) years.

"For count two, for Assault with Intent to Rob Armed, the Court will impose a sentence of life. And for count three, Possession of a Firearm in Commission of a Felony, the Court will sentence him to two years consecutive.

"Now, since this is a Habitual 4 Offender, the Court will set aside that sentence. Habitual 4 Offenders have no guidelines. The court is going to sentence him for Assault with Intent to Commit Murder to serve a sentence of seventy-five (75) to one hundred fifty (150) years.

"The Court will sentence him to serve life for Assault with Intent to Commit Robbery; and will sentence him to serve two years consecutive for Possession of a Firearm in Commission of a Felony. He will serve out his current sentence, and then he will begin serving this one.

"The Court does regret that Michigan has no death penalty, because under the circumstances, the Court wouldn't hesitate to impose it."

As the Aspen County Deputies were escorting him back to the holding cell, Arthur Wideman hollered, "I'm still going to do what I said I was going to do."

Fortunately for me, this was the last time I was going to have to see him.

Relieved the trial was over; my family escorted me down the back elevator to avoid contact with the defendant's family. They were abusive. His mother shouted at me, saying, "That woman's lying. You know you're lying. We're going to go and get a *real* lawyer and win this case."

29

Fizzled Out

All the pieces of the puzzle fit. My theory about the shooting was this: that funny feeling I'd had in my gut after Mr. Malone left on December 8, 1992 was valid. I told my supervisor, Grace Jackson, about that feeling. Mr. Malone's anger was scary. Her advice was good. She told me to update the file and ask for a warrant for violation of probation.

I updated the file, but I didn't have time to seek the warrant. In fact, I never saw my complete file again. All the incriminating evidence was gone. The arrogant Mr. Malone, the drug dealer, had won. To do it, he injured me and bought off a few people. Now, to make matters worse, they freed him to return to *my supervision.* He had already destroyed my health, and now it was getting worse. I won in court, but I was not winning with my employer. *The man, who shot me, was not going to spend a day in prison.*

Supervised by me? I don't think so! The judge removed him from the high-risk program back to me? It boggled my fragile state of mind. How unfair!

I tried to treat everybody fair. I could not believe the way my career was going awry. Since when did the bad guys win and the good guys lose? I had found the guilty party and given him over to our justice system to handle.

Now, Mr. Malone was getting away with attempted murder. Without the testimony of Mr. Wideman, there was no concrete evidence connecting him to the crime. The anonymous caller's words were not admissible in a court of law, but I knew a court that was always in session and justice was always fair. *God* saw what this man did.

I was sure the day would come, either on Earth or in Heaven for him to be held accountable for the shooting. Even if punishment didn't come until Judgment Day, it was all right with me. But he would pay. I wondered where was he going to spend his eternity.

One June 23, 1993, I reported to work as directed, but the day didn't begin too well. My memory replayed the defendant's threat, and what the anonymous caller told me on the phone. The two together caused me to dread going back to work. Usually I arrived at work early, entering the building with no other employees nearby.

I was too afraid to go in early that day, so I waited until the last moment to arrive so I could join the crowd of co-workers. I must have been too late because I found myself alone again, trying to get my key into the back door's lock. I was so nervous that I fumbled, and dropped the keys on the ground. That just intensified the fear. Finally, I stuck the key in the door and it opened. I signed in with tears streaming down my cheeks.

Lillian asked, "Denise, what's wrong?"

I whispered, "I can't do this any more."

I went to my office and let the floodgates flow. Then I found my supervisor and said, "I'm sorry, but this is my last day on this job."

She asked, "Can you make it through the day?"

"Yes, I think so."

Alarmed, she started calling to find out what to do. I was walking on the edge of a nervous breakdown. I tried my best to implement some crisis intervention for myself. I made appointments with my doctor and my psychologist. Then I went to pack my personal items from my desk. I wasn't sure if I would ever pass through those doors again. I needed time to pray and think it over.

I finally found the job-related connection to the shooting. It frightened me.

So, what was I to do?

As the sun set on my life, as I knew it, I began a journey to the dark side. The opaque canvas of despair swallowed up the light of hope. I avoided this place for many years. I escorted many people from the edge of this mental state. I didn't want a home in that hellhole. But now I confirmed my reservation—and moved all my belongings in—for an indefinite stay at Hotel Doom and Gloom.

I didn't want to leave, but the more I resisted the deeper I sank into the sinking sand of hopelessness.

Now, black darkness enveloped my life like a tidal wave that overtakes an unsuspecting surfer. During my waking hours, sadness engulfed me. While I slept, I dreamed of violence and despair. Violence and sadness invaded every crevice of my mind. The unwanted intruder, blackness, grabbed hold of me and refused to let go.

Searching for at least a flicker of light, I turned to the Word of God. I trusted the Holy Spirit's guidance and encouragement to guide me back to the light. So doing, I began to chisel away at the darkness that contended for my soul.

Finally, I accepted my fate. All the flickering lights dimmed until they were no more. The inner voices of protest quieted. I had no more strength with which to contend with the opponent. I threw the towel of Hope into the ring, and called off the fight, surrendering to hopelessness.

At first, it was peaceful. I slept as long as I wanted without interference. No alarm clocks, no reports to write, no expectations from anyone. I didn't have to be afraid anymore.

I was safe in my house and no intruder was going to cross the threshold of my refuge. It was good to feel *safe*. What I didn't realize was that the strings of hopelessness were wrapping around my soul. Each day I basked in the safety of my refuge, yet fear of the unknown tortured me. Tomorrow's challenges were too much to even think about.

Unanswered questions tossed around in my mind.

Who was I now? What would I become? How would I provide for my family?

These questions invaded my solitude. They changed from being simple questions to being my accusers.

You're nothing. You will never be anything.

Guilt and shame were my companions. They asked questions like, *How can you leave your family in a financial bind?*

The phrases ought to, should have, would have, and could have all chimed in with guilt and shame.

Shame on you! You should have fought this darkness. It would have been better if you took the bribe. At least you'd still be working.

The voices all spoke at once, spinning my thoughts as though in a funnel cloud, around and around like the winds of a tornado. The debris of self-pity, doubt, fear and anger whirled and twirled about, leaving me dizzy and lost.

Where do I go from here?

I wandered away from *me*, didn't know how to get back, and was a long way from the *me* before the shooting.

In just one year I had become physically challenged from a work injury, single, and a statistic of urban violence. The injury, and becoming a victim of crime, finally cost me my career. I wanted to discover my God ordained purpose, not the new foreign person. The transition hurt and it was scary. This journey was on the pathways of the slippery slopes of uncharted territory. The unknown was the scariest part of the trip.

Would the sun ever shine on my life again? Or would the darkness overtake me? Could I hang onto my belief in God? Or was I a phony? Was I a fair-weather Christian who fainted at the first signs of misfortune?

And I needed to ask the final questions: *Who am I? Do I believe what I preach and teach?*

30

The Slippery Slope of Hopelessness

If I rested, I could get myself together and return to work. I thought the melancholy was temporary and that in no time at all I would be back to work.

One month passed, and another began, and I was worse instead of better. I had no money, because the disability papers kept getting lost. My children were spending their court-ordered summer vacation with their father. On the day of their return I had neither money nor food. I cried and cried. I couldn't take care of my family. The day before the children were to arrive home, Aetna, my disability carrier, approved the claim.

My friend, Barry, tried to soothe my anguish, saying, "If I have a biscuit, you will, too."

I appreciated his kindness. I knew he meant it. I never relied on other people's generosity, and didn't want to start. Also, I didn't want his conditional generosity. Could I afford to pay the price?

The kids were to arrive home by six o'clock, and I still had not received a check. However, I was still trying to hold onto faith that a check would arrive in time.

God once told me: *I am always on time.*

Now, He asked me: *When do you need the money?*

I said: "Today by six."

"He said: *Is it six?*"

"No."

Then, I am not late.

Frustrated, I gathered my scraps of faith and believed that something was going to happen that day. I waited for the mail carrier, sitting in the window. That afternoon the mail arrived at 12:40 and in the mail was an envelope from Aetna, my disability carrier. I had a check. It would buy groceries and take care of some other needs.

Hallelujah. God had been on time.

However, I had the nerve to ask God: "Didn't You cut that a little close? Couldn't You have sent it sooner?"

He asked, *"When did you need it?"*

I answered: "By six o'clock"

"What time did it arrive?"

"Twelve-forty."

"Then I was on time."

God had a point; He did what I had asked Him to do. It was up to me to do my part. Now, I needed to shake loose from depression, and get into action. I needed to go to the bank and cash the check and buy groceries. I washed up, put on some clothes, and went to the bank.

Once there, I ran into an obstacle. I could deposit my check but could not access the funds for seven days. My bank's policy, for out of town checks, was to hold the funds until it cleared. Desperate, since I didn't have the time to wait for the funds to clear, I started praying a quick, silent prayer for favor with the bank manager.

As I waited my turn to see her, I prayed: "Lord, You wouldn't bring me so close now, would You, and then not meet my needs?"

The silence made me believe His answer was no. I looked up, as the manager appeared, saying: "Denise Thomason, may I help you?"

"Oh, yes, please, if you would. Here is a disability check from a Boston bank, and the teller told me that I had to wait to negotiate the funds."

"Correct."

"Miss, I don't have time to wait."

I explained to her my circumstances, and about the shooting.

She listened intently, then said: "I'll tell you what, we'll hold a portion of the funds, and allow you to take enough to buy groceries. Will that help?"

My heart leaped for joy as I took my money and bought food. Right on schedule, at six o'clock the children trooped in. I was so *glad* to see them. And they were glad to be home with a refrigerator full of food. They always loved grocery day, and so had I. They had no idea that only a few hours before, there was no food.

To this day, I'm grateful for God's intervention. That miracle gave me needed strength to keep on believing the impossible. However, my thoughts still weren't getting any better. My self-talk was sounding worse and worse each day, and I was beginning to identify with the violence in the news.

I understood now why a factory worker could go to work and shoot up his boss. Or, why a daughter who lost her mother to cancer took a gun to Henry Ford Hospital and shot and killed the doctor. This was a little scary.

Some days, I turned the anger against me and felt that everyone would be better if I were dead. I felt that my employer, especially, would be happy.

I shared these thoughts with my friend La Dean, who told me "I don't like what I'm hearing. Please, won't you see my doctor? I've never had any confidence in your psychologist—she allowed you to return to work too soon. You need a psychiatrist who deals with diseases of the mind."

I trusted her. We had been friends for almost 20 years. We'd seen each other through some hard times, so I made the appointment to see Dr. Jorge Zuniga (fondly called Dr. Z), who listened for an hour. He listened, unaffected by my craziness. I liked him.

He said, "I need to see you for four consecutive weeks before I can adequately assess you."

I looked forward to those meetings. At last, I could get better. By the fourth meeting, he recommended that I not return to work. He also recommended that I enroll in a Day Hospital Program at Margaret Montgomery, a hospital for psychiatric treatment.

Only Dr. Z could make such a recommendation seem like a trip to a resort. He told me "This will help you gain more coping skills. It will be an immediate intervention to stop your violent, suicidal, and obsessive thoughts."

I looked him in the eye and said, "Well…as long as I can go home every day, I'll do it. I don't want to lose my children."

I was always afraid that if any one knew my thoughts, they would take away my children. However, I felt that this doctor would not betray my confidence.

I imagined people walking around the hospital talking to themselves, as in the Northville Regional Psychiatric Hospital in Plymouth, Michigan. I had gone many times to this hospital as a probation officer to check records. It was not a place I wanted to visit, but Margaret Montgomery Hospital was not like that. It wasn't a resort, but it was tolerable.

31

Detoured

All mental health professionals are not the same. Some labor for the paycheck, others want to help. Dr. Zuniga is the latter, a helpful psychiatrist. He considers all the circumstances surrounding a patient. He has a good memory, too. If not memory, then he keeps good notes. From my first meeting, I liked him; but I didn't necessarily trust him. He had to earn that. Enough people had disappointed me already, so he wasn't going to get my trust without proving himself.

He was from Lima, Peru, spoke several languages, and enjoyed playing musical instruments. He brought his zest for life into the session, and this enticed me to find my own zeal to get well. I liked how he pinpointed my strengths and steered me back toward what I had, not what I lost.

As we talked, he learned that I liked to write. Writing was part of my job, but at home I kept a journal, and this kept me sane. The journal housed my thoughts.

"Someday," I told him, "I'm going to write a book."

"Good," he replied. "Bring in your manuscripts and let me read them."

So, as time went on and I began the book, he would read my excerpts and encourage me to continue writing.

For a long time, I tried to return to work. Dr. Z never discouraged me from trying. However, he would caution me not to run too fast. He had clients who went through less than I had who still hadn't left their homes. He wanted me to pat myself on the back for my progress. I hated my disability, and he knew it. He also wanted me to understand the steps to wholeness and not try to set an unhealthy deadline.

Eventually, I had to take Zoloft, an anti-depressant. It took a long time for me to accept this, since I believed that a Christian didn't need it. All I had to do was pray and believe God, and that would heal me.

However, healing was not coming as quickly as I wanted, so I eventually took the blue pill. My body fought against the effects for awhile. Then one day, I could think a little better, and the swirling thoughts were not as erratic. Zoloft is a serotonin re-uptake inhibitor drug, which decreases sadness tendencies and helps one to see the sunnier side of life.

Dr. Z would get me to take Zoloft—first, if, I didn't gain weight from it. Second, if it didn't affect my personality. Third, if I could stop at anytime without a withdrawal. It turned out to meet all needs. However, the drug irritated my colon and my urinary tract, causing diarrhea and incontinence, which made life miserable. Nevertheless, it did stabilize my emotions. It freed Saun to move out and find a place of her own.

Also, sending me to Margaret Montgomery for outpatient mental health care helped to speed up my recovery. Just the thought of outpatient treatment made me fearful. Most of us fear the unknown; I was no different.

Who was going to see me? What would people think if they knew? What would my church family think if they knew what was going on?

I tried to resign, as Director of Children's Church, but Bishop David Ellis would only agree to a leave of absence; and my assistant temporarily took over my duties.

The first day was the hardest. My thoughts ran wild.

How did my life come to this—disabled and mentally ill? How did a probation officer, preacher, and child of God wind up in a place like this?

The answer was easy. Somebody shot me and I was not adjusting well to that fact. I felt like a dinosaur; he was extinct and so was I. No one understood my plight, and that was as good as it was going to get.

To my surprise, the hospital turned out to be a decent place. People were friendly and helpful. There were a few exceptions, but overall they were as normal as I was. Some were angry; some scared, most just wanted to make sense of what they were going through. Some had terminal illnesses, such as Lou Gehrig's Disease, that would eventually bring death.

We were all rather young, all trying to have a normal life, and somehow, that wasn't happening as fast as we wanted. Our mental problems were causing other ones, such as marital problems, sleeping difficulties, and other symptoms of stress.

After that first day, I loved it. Here were people who understood what I was going through. They didn't spiritualize it. They took a hard look at the problem and made some practical suggestions.

Al, the psychologist assigned to my group therapy, was one cool 'brother.' He was a tall, slender, African-American man who was real and down to earth. He wore vintage suits that he bought from re-sale shops, and he must have splashed some sweet-smelling cologne on every day. His vintage Stacey Adams shoes where spit-shine bright and he didn't talk to us like we were crazy. In fact, he wouldn't tolerate it. He was about self-empowerment.

He said, "You will get out of group therapy what you invest. It's up to you how fast you grow."

He made us responsible for our own growth, and I liked that. He also prodded us at times to *get off our seats of doing nothing and get in the game of getting better.*

I can only remember a couple of strange people. One had had the tip of his nose bitten off by a dog. Turned out, he'd stared at a dog, nose to nose, and started barking at the dog. The dog didn't like this little gesture, and bit off the tip of his nose. Can you believe this man wanted to be my boyfriend? I declined, since I had given up on men. He didn't give up easily, but eventually he had to believe that I meant no.

Of course, I was still having a weird friendship with Barry, who was stressful and confusing. So, I didn't need a certifiable crazy person to add to my world.

The other strange person was a woman who was an inpatient, upgraded to outpatient status with us. She had a bad day when she kept hearing voices telling her to kill herself. The doctors increased her medicine, but it didn't help. One woman told her to fight it, saying, "It ain't nothing but them demons."

I started pleading the blood of Jesus and told her, "Girl, call on the name of Jesus. He can help you."

However, our advice was no help since this was a repetitive episode with her.

One day, the nurse took her out in the hallway and we never saw her again. They had to re-admit her for her own safety.

Group therapy and individual sessions with Dr. Z helped the most. The classes we had to take also gave us tools to grow. Staff members identified issues like depression. They told us what it was, why some people get it, why others are able to avoid it, and how we could help ourselves get well.

We took a class on anger. It was helpful to most of us. Most of us were having some court battle and angered by that. It was there, in the hospital, that I received the best advice from the patients themselves who testified to both the right and wrong ways to handle anger and authority.

They shared with me that if I let the emotion of anger rule me; I was going to lose my court case. Further, focusing on the mistreatment from my employer would only irritate my circumstances. I needed to learn that I have the power to trust God and wait until my change came. It was almost a guarantee that I would win.

The group adopted me as their special case. They felt that my employer was wrong to assign me to unnecessary dangers. They also assured me that God was on my side, and if I could keep patience and not let anger rule, that I would win my case. One of the most violent persons there gave me the best advice about anger, and to this day it has benefited me whenever I'm about to lose my composure.

32

Stop the Madness

I didn't complete my visits at Margaret Montgomery, after my gynecologist, Dr. Shea, found a mass on my right ovary.

She said, "You need immediate surgery. It looks like ovarian cancer; and if not treated early, you can die."

She also found an abdominal hernia. During physical therapy I pulled loose the repaired lining in my stomach, and both of these conditions needed surgery.

This was a real setback. When I got home, I fell onto my bed crying, "Oh, God. Please, no more surgery. And I don't want to go under ether again. I'm tired of folks cutting on me. I just had surgery in June to remove the last bullet."

They found all but one with the first surgery, but in June 1993, they found the last one.

Now, the doctor told me that my right ovary had to come out since it had a cyst on it. She was not sure if it would be a total hysterectomy, but she was grave and sorry that this was happening to me.

When I telephoned my prayer partner, Sandra, and told her that my doctor said I was facing another surgery, she proposed a plan that she knew would work.

"Why don't we pray on Thursday for the surgery on the next Tuesday? We can send prayers through time and set up the day that you want."

She began to pray: "Dear God, we trust You to go with Denise on Tuesday and give her peace. She needs to rest in Your hands and understand that You have everything under control. You will be in charge of her from the beginning of the day to her discharge from the hospital."

She continued: "We're asking a special request. Please go to the infected spot and heal the cancer. You are the Master Surgeon. If it is Your will, we ask that you remove it. Your child has been through enough. We ask that You take care of every part of her. Guide the surgeon's hands; and please be with the anesthesiologist, that he does not over-medicate her. You know she has a strange chemical balance in her body. And, God, please don't allow the medication to weaken her hair. We ask this all in Jesus' name, Amen."

Her prayer enlightened me. I didn't know that we could ask God to go through time and fix a situation ahead of time. The prayer put me at ease.

Sniffing back tears, I told her, "Sandra, thanks. I feel that God has everything under control. I can face it now."

On Tuesday, my parents took me to the hospital. Mom went in the prep room with me. She said, "Denise, your skin is glowing. You look so pretty and relaxed."

Somehow, I couldn't stop singing praise songs. I sang so much the staff commented on how soothing the songs were and how relaxed I was.

The most gentle staff people surrounded me. My primary doctor, Dr. Shea, was from India. Nearly her entire team was from India or of Asian descent, and they gave me the best care I had ever experienced. The second doctor, a plastic surgeon, was also from India, and he was to repair the hernia.

He introduced himself and shook my hand.

"My name is Dr. Ramon Tuli. Now, Denise, I'm going to explain the procedure so you'll understand what's going on. We'll get you fixed up, and you'll soon be home."

He seemed honored to help in the surgery. This doctor's bedside manner was so soothing. He had salt and pepper hair, so I knew that he wasn't a novice. He knew what he was doing. After the entire introduction, they put me to sleep, and I relaxed knowing that God had everything under control.

After surgery, the nurses took me to my room. My bandaged belly let me know that I had major surgery. I wanted to know what organs the doctor removed. It looked like it did when I'd came out of surgery for the bullets, but there was one comfort—there weren't as many tubes.

Over in the other bed I saw a familiar face. It was Teresa, a woman who had gone to our church for about five years, though I hadn't seen her in about ten.

"Hey, Girl, what are you doing in here?"

"Denise," she said, raising her head from the pillow, "is that you? Girl, I saw you talk about the shooting on television. I felt so bad to see that happen to you. What are you doing in here now?" Not waiting for me to answer, she went on, "Girl, my doctor was afraid that I had cancer—and I did—so they had to do a total hysterectomy."

When I got the chance to speak, I said, "I don't know what they did to me, since I haven't seen my doctor yet. I know they were to remove my right ovary, and she needs to tell me what else."

Teresa was upset, and let it all hang out. Cervical cancer ran in her family, so she'd had a total hysterectomy. She was also having trouble in her marriage, so her life was in a mess. She admitted that she was mad at God, so my stay involved ministering to Teresa. She needed an ear, and I was it.

Dr. Shea came the following day.

"Doc, so what all did you take out?"

"Don't let anyone give you a laproscopy of the abdomen. It's a mess in there. I had trouble even finding your ovaries. When they put your body parts back in, they must have *thrown* them in. It was hard to find your organs. You had so many adhesions that we had to go in and clean them up," Dr. Shea said.

She cleared her throat and went on: "It appears that what I saw on the X-rays were adhesions. I did not physically see your ovaries, but I felt them. They were of normal proportions and healthy. I cleaned up as many adhesions as I could and got out of there."

It took a moment to let that news sink in.

"Let me understand what you're saying. *I have 26 stitches in my gut for nothing?*"

"No, we cleaned up the adhesions."

"No cancer?"

"No."

I should have been grateful, but I already was in a delicate mental state and didn't take the news well. It was a good thing the surgeon, Dr. Tuli, who repaired the hernia, came soon after the gynecologist. He came in to talk about the marvelous job that he did.

Dr. Tuli said: "I gave you back your belly button. I took that old scar out and put in a narrower line. I took your stomach and reshaped it after I did the hernia repair. How do you like it?"

I was so excited about getting my navel back that I forgot about the ovarian cancer scare. This was bringing me back to some normalcy. I hated the botched up stomach they left me with. Now I had a stomach that looked normal. It was worth one more surgery.

"I like it, Doc. You do good work."

When he left, I had a little talk with God.

"Why'd You let me go through unnecessary surgery for cancer?"

What makes you think that it wasn't there?

What was that? Did God perform the surgery before the doctors had a chance?

33

Beautiful Side of Evil

My first real try at romance, in 1994, did not go well, so I included this story as an example of how the shooting affected my thinking.

When I needed to learn good courting skills, I sought the wisdom of my pastor. I asked, "What should a single person do in this crazy dating world, and remain celibate?"

He told me: "You will have to pray about it. I can't give you much advice since I haven't been single in a long time. If something happens to Mother Ellis, I will remarry. I believe she will out-live me, so I can't help you."

With that advice I went out of his office, trying to find a way through the maze of my confusion and hormones. I think I wore a sign on me that read, "Needy," since it appeared that I was still attracting more takers and unhealthy people who used me.

In January 1994, I went to watch my son Adam play in a basketball tournament. He was on the team for Hally Middle School, and this particular day he was playing against the #1 team, Shallom Middle School, whose coach was Sherman Tiller. He looked from a distance like a chocolate Super Fly, or maybe a Nick Ashford "wanna-be" with black, shoulder length hair.

His team of skilled young men responded to his coaching, and pulverized our guys. When the game was over, we were all thankful, and I stayed to see the other teams play.

Sherman Tiller and his team took the stands, receiving congratulations on a job well done. Shortly after that, I began to feel his eyes looking at me. I ignored him. At half time, Coach Tiller came over and sat down next to me.

He said: "Did you see my team play?"

"Yes."

"So, what did you think of it?"

"It was a good game. Your guys beat us bad."

He gave a low, deep chuckle and said, "Yeah, we did, didn't we?" Then he introduced himself, saying, "My name is Sherman Tiller, and yours?"

"Denise."

I couldn't believe that I was talking to Super Fly himself.

"Does that first name have a last name?"

"Yes," I blushed. "It's Thomason."

"Well, Denise Thomason, I would like to know you better. Are you married?"

"No."

"Neither am I. I am good for a date and a dinner. Can I get your number?"

"I don't think so."

"I tell you what. I'll give you my card with my number, and if you reconsider, call me and we will set up a date."

He smiled at me, and I noted that Super Fly had a handsome, seductive smile. He didn't look bad up close, either. I like African-American men with a dark hue to their skin and a beautiful smile. He had both a beard and a mustache to add to his charm. His charm tempted me. I wanted to check him out. I rationalized that he could be a good Christian, but I would never know until I dialed the number.

Watch it, I thought. *This guy's coming on strong.*

At last, I said, "Okay," and took the card.

This man's warmth and clever introduction haunted me. I caught myself smiling when there was no reason. My lust made me want to taste forbidden fruit. He was one of those types Mom warned me about. She called them "Slick Cats". Like Eve, in the Bible I had let him talk, and now I was curious.

Should I bite?

I let a few days pass, then called him.

He said, "I know who you are, and I'm surprised you called."

I made some excuse for calling, and we chitchatted for a while. Then we decided to have our first date. He played for the Board of Education bowling team, so I met him at the lanes. He was a good bowler. So far this man excelled at everything he did. I was a little intimidated. Was this a character trait that should send me running?

He introduced me to everyone. I felt special. He wasn't afraid for others to see me associating with him. I was his woman that night, and it was a good feeling.

Sherman was a gentleman. He offered to buy me dinner at a greasy spoon restaurant, but since grease sent my intestines into spasms I passed on our first meal together.

That Friday night, he wanted to see me again. The kids were with their dad for the weekend and I was all by myself. This was looking good. Two dates in one week.

This time we went to a skating rink, another place he attended weekly. Since I was still recovering from surgeries, I couldn't even think about putting on a skate, so I watched him all night go 'round and 'round again. He was wearing biker shorts that were skin tight, a tank top that showed all his rock hard muscles and sweat—and his bulging calves pushed up out of his skates. He'd stop every so often to check on me and take a rest.

In time, I learned that Sherman knew how to find women who were desperate. He became their comforter. In me, Sherman had seen a needy woman and offered his services. He once told me that he wondered what his purpose was for me. He believed God sent me to him so he could teach me something. (I think it was to learn to be wary of wolves in sheep's clothing.)

The Bible says in 2 Timothy 3:6, *For of this sort are they which creep into houses, and lead captive silly women laden with sins, led away with divers lusts....*

He was a charmer. He did help me to forget the self-pity in which I wallowed. We would talk and eat, but I found he had other appetites too. He was fattening me up for the kill and he was good at what he did. He loved the company of women. He loved the chase and the hunt, but left empty in the end. I learned that his heart couldn't feel the warmth of a woman, just his flesh.

He once told me that his first wife hurt him bad. He purposed in his heart that no one else was going to do that to him. I identified with him. In fact, before he came along I was trying to put my heart under lock and key, never to be vulnerable to love again. On that day, as we talked, a strange event happened. His eyes looked like vacant holes that penetrated deep into the depths of his soul.

A still, small voice said, *"He has no light. If you harden your heart you will be just like him."*

God knew how to spoil a moment. From then on, Sherman was not as exciting to be with. In fact, I started seeing him differently. He never wanted to do anything that I wanted to do. He did not court like a gentleman. He also wanted to isolate me from my children. He made promises that he did not keep. I found that it was a one-sided friendship; I was there for his pleasure when he had time.

The children saw through his façade. Out of the mouths of babes came much wisdom.

Aaron, the oldest said, "Mom, why are you going out with that guy anyway?"

Angela chimed in; "He's creepy."

Adam laughed. "I can't believe that you are going out with the coach from Shallom Middle School.

They were not the only people who weren't happy. Sandra was upset. She had never met him, but she judged him through what I said when rattling on about my new beau.

"Girl, he scares me. He is too smooth and has no restraints. I am going to pray. I just don't trust him with you."

Saun pleaded, "Nisey, just let me know where you are and when you are going. Chally and I will come and kick his butt if he mistreats you."

Chally agreed. "You know we got your back. No one will come break up the Three Musketeers. Sometimes I am not sure if we are more like the Three Stooges. Whatever, we'll do whatever we have to do to keep you safe."

Then one day God thundered, *Break it off! I've had this man's real nature under My control, but when you see him from now on, you will see another man. Turn around.*

At first I was sad. Then I became afraid.

What did God mean that he changed his real nature? Is he abusive and not kind? Is he a rapist or, worse, a murderer? Who is this man that I invited into my life?

Obediently and notably shaken, I called Sherman to set up a time to break off the friendship. Those were the longest seven numbers I have ever dialed.

Ring…Ring…Ring…This is Sherman; leave a message.

I got his answering machine.

Shoot, he's not at home. I didn't want to speak to his answering machine. Before I lose my nerve I better leave a message.

"This is Denise, call me when you get in. I have an urgent matter I need to discuss with you."

It was some time before he returned my call, and we set up a tentative time for me to meet him at his house between Sunday church services. When I arrived there, he was not home.

I went and sat in my car and waited in front of his house. And waited and *waited.* At last, I went to the pay phone, called again, and was making one last sweep of his block when I saw his pimp mobile, an old navy blue Lincoln Continental, ease on down the street.

He didn't stop at his house, but at his neighbor's. I waited for a minute to see what was going on. He had a woman in the car with him. I backed my car up a few houses and waited to see the outcome.

Eventually, he drove home with that woman still in the car. Once there, he and the woman jumped out of the car and went into his house without seeing me. Soon, he stormed out of the house like a raging lion. Something or someone made him angry.

Someone else was his prey, but, judging from his looks, I'd better get out of there. Through the window I could see the woman making herself comfortable on the sofa. She didn't look as though she needed my pity.

The two-timing dog! I thought to myself. He never takes that long to return my call. Hmmm...I don't see what he sees in her any way. She isn't even cute. Now I see, this is what God was trying to warn me about.

Trembling, I went on to church, thanking God for His goodness and kindness. He warned me, and now I had seen Sherman's ravenous spirit and total lack of commitment to any woman, including me.

It hurt. But most of all, I was feeling stupid.

Why did I date him anyway?

Somehow, in my loneliness, I lost the warning signals. Like a deer drawn to headlights, I stared at trouble and then walked toward it. Although I was living in an upside down world, God was there all the time and never stopped talking to me. I just had trouble distinguishing which voice to follow.

34

God's Rescue Team

Even though I was thankful that God protected me from Sherman, I was sad that we were not together any more. He was company. He filled in the lonely hours when the children went to their dad's every other weekend. Separated from the children twice a month made my heart ache, a forced separation didn't seem fair. They were my reasons for living.

The children kept my mind from hearing those voices of accusation and disappointment.

How could you violate the ten commandments like that? Thou shall not fornicate. So you call yourself a Christian? God can't use you now. You blew it. You will never preach another anointed message. Look at you, you are all washed up. Anointed prophetess...who, you? I don't think so.

These are the conversations that repeated themselves in my mind, day in and day out.

Although guilt and shame were my companions, I also carried with me their archenemies, Mercy and Grace. They would soothe my pain. Grace would comfort me by saying, "God is not afraid of dirt, you are. He is not looking for perfection. He took any sin that you could commit to the cross already."

Mercy would chime in and say, "He already paid the price and the penalty for your sin."

"It is no use, I said. I am useless. I am a bad person and a poor excuse for a Christian."

"No, you, are not," cried Mercy.

"God, can't forgive this," I cried.

"Then you have missed the reason Christ died on the cross," replied Grace.

I was hard on myself. I could help others accept God's mercy, but somehow I could not receive it. One day God called me to Him in a small, comforting voice.

Denise, why do you reject me?

"What? I am not rejecting you, God. I am not worthy because of what I have done."

Turn to II Kings 5 and read about Naaman, a captain of the Syrian army.

"I know the story. But, God, I don't have leprosy."

It is about my dealing with what's unclean in your life. Apply the principles and you will see that it is the same.

Opening my Bible, I turned to 2 Kings 5:1. I began reading. *Now Naaman, captain of the host of the king of Syria, was a great man with his master, and honourable, because by him the Lord had given deliverance unto Syria: he was also a mighty man in valour, but he was a leper.*

I knew this story. He had integrity, fearlessness, and favor of God and man. His reputation went before his sickness. God gave him preferential treatment despite the leprosy. His uncleanness did not stop his victories in battles.

He wasn't in the nation of Israel. He wasn't trying to serve God. He was a heathen to whom God gave favor.

I began to think.

Hmmm...I am at least in covenant with God through Jesus Christ. If he could show favor to Naaman perhaps I still have a chance for redemption.

Reading on, there was a captive slave girl in his household who suggested the God of Israel could heal him. He took the suggestion and sought healing. In his pride, Naaman wanted healing his way. To Naaman's surprise, he didn't get the results sought until he humbled himself and was obedient to God's word given to him from the prophet Elisha.

Elisha's, servant Gehazi, told this warrior to go to the Jordan River and dip seven times. Sounds simple, but Jordan was a polluted body of water. It looked as if it would cause more disease than it would cure.

Naaman's first response was: "No." It didn't make sense and he wasn't doing it.

"Why didn't he ask me to dip in the other bodies of water in Damascus that were clean and not polluted?" He asked.

Wasn't that the logical way to receive his healing? Perhaps, but God didn't follow his logic. He set up these circumstances to defy man's logic and the glory would only go to Him.

His servant said, "If God had asked you to do some great feat you would have done it willingly. Why do you resist this simple task?"

When healing became more important than his pride, Naaman followed the instructions. As directed, he dipped seven times. He received his healing on the seventh time he emerged from the water. His skin was smooth like a baby's. Naaman received total deliverance. He was a mature man with aged, diseased skin. God made the stinky, sewage waters, from the polluted Jordan River become a fountain of youth. Restoration was better than he had expected. God gave him a youthful, dewy, appearance.

God convinced Naaman that the God of Israel was the true God. He no longer had his physical sickness or his spiritual blindness. God healed him, spirit, soul, and body. Pride changed to humility and he began to worship the true and living God of Israel.

Logic and pride blocked his healing initially. He wanted the royal treatment. He turned his back on his deliverance. It sounds dumb, but it made sense, to him, at the time. Thank God for his mercy. In God's wisdom he sent another servant, who had courage to challenge his master's decision not to heed what the prophet said. That rebuke humbled Naaman. The humility that followed led to his compliance and his healing.

God's mercy dealt with his attitude, his devotions, pride and spiritual sickness. God wanted to perform that same miracle for me.

35

All Shook Up

As everyone knows, living with three teenagers is not easy. They didn't talk much about the shooting, but it came out in their behavior. They seemed vulnerable, perhaps in fear of losing me, perhaps frightened of the future or their own safety.

Financially, we did well. Long-term disability provided an income for two years. Then, in April 1995, I received my last disability check, and for seven months we had no income.

I applied for Worker's Compensation and Social Security; they both denied me. My family helped. The church and well wishers gave money out of compassion, and every so often a child support check came in.

Angie was working at Tradewinds Video Store, so she provided some income when she could. Our finances looked bleak. I thought one more problem would shatter my mind.

My "play niece," Gorie, a cosmetologist, tried to cheer me up. She would give me gorgeous hairstyles to make me feel better. She called me auntie.

"Auntie, want me to get rid of the gray and make you look good?"

"Yes." I replied.

This particular day she did just that. I wanted to show off my new look, so, I went to see Angie at her job. She wasn't there. A little alarmed, I went to a few of her hangouts and couldn't find her. More alarmed, I called her friend, Keisha, and her boyfriend, Jeff. Neither try was successful.

I went home and grabbed the telephone. Just when I was ready to push the panic button, she walked in.

"Where have you been?" I screamed, unable to keep my cool.

"Nowhere."

"What do you mean, nowhere? You had to be somewhere. You weren't at work and nobody's seen you. I went by the store to show you my new hairdo, and you weren't there."

I couldn't stop screaming.

Angie just looked out the window with a blank stare and refused to answer.

"Angie, tell me—where have you been?"

Finally, in an undertone, she confessed: "I was with my boyfriend, Jeff."

I sure wasn't in a mood for sass that night. As I shouted, "Where?" She dropped the bomb.

"Since you don't like me right now, anyway, I might as well tell you that I'm pregnant."

"You're *what?*" My stomach lurched.

"Pregnant."

"How many months?"

"Four."

"Why did you wait so long to tell me?"

"I wanted to decide what I was going to do. Now, I've decided I'm going to have this baby."

Hurt and angry, I wanted to run as far from her as possible. But mothers can't do that. Mothers have to do what they can to salvage a bad choice. The worst of it was, I'd just had a conversation with both Angie and her boyfriend, and had told him that this was my only daughter and I didn't want him messing over her.

"Look, I don't want her coming up pregnant." I told them. "You're older, already out of high school, and I'm wondering why you're dating my daughter?"

He shrugged.

"I like dating her. What's wrong with that?"

Angie had piped in with, "Look, Mom, this is embarrassing. Just leave us alone? I love Jeff and that's that."

It was obvious that forbidding her to see him wasn't going to work, so I had tried compromise.

Now, I smacked my hand to my forehead.

Well, duh. Why hadn't I seen this coming?

We'd just gone shopping for her homecoming dress, which was skin-tight. No way could a four-month pregnant stomach have gone unnoticed, but it had.

Pained, I realized I was almost the last one to know.

And so the drama unfurled. There was no money to feed *us*. How would we feed another mouth? She needed prenatal care. The doctor discovered two infections, one in her blood that was turning her skin gray. It frightened me.

What about the baby?

The doctor had to be conservative with medication because she was pregnant.

Next, as she was driving to school, she ran into a car that stopped in front of her, and tore up the front end of her car. It meant a trip to the emergency room, but she received a clean bill of health. A few hours later, Angie went into premature labor. She woke me up complaining about having trouble sleeping. She described abdominal contractions three minutes apart.

Good. I thought as she crawled into the bed next to me. *A miscarriage would solve most of our problems. Maybe it's God's way of dealing with this.* It was sad, though, because Angie had already named the baby Nathan.

Then she said, "Mom, I love Nathan. I don't want anything to happen to him."

My heart ached for her. "Come here, let me pray for you."

I talked to her belly, "Father, in the name of Jesus, You already know this baby by name. He's trying to come before his time, and only

You can calm him down and put him to sleep so he won't come for another five months."

I'd read a report that said babies could hear what is going on outside the stomach wall. It was worth a shot. So, I began singing: *Jesus loves the little children, all the children of the world. Red and yellow, black and white, they are precious in His sight. Jesus loves the little children of the world.*

Then I spoke to Nathan, personally.

"Nathan, I know that you are in a hurry to see all of us, but this is not the time. Go to sleep and wait until it's time."

Through this whole time of prayer, Angie fell asleep and—apparently, so did Nathan. He didn't come until five months later, a full-term baby boy. Thank God for His mercy.

As I thought about it, perhaps Angie's need to have a boyfriend had something to do with her father's absence. He married another woman, who sealed off the prospects of his ever coming home; two months before Angie told me she was pregnant.

Also, her oldest brother, Aaron, left for Oregon State University the month before her Dad remarried, which meant that both of her dominant male figures were absent. Aaron was much too far away for us to visit.

Lord, I thought, *what happened? This precious daughter who just had a Sweet Sixteen Party, who is on the honor roll at Cass Technical, in her last year of high school, and accepted already at universities—is pregnant. Not only that, she has just finished a course at Barbizon Modeling school. How will pregnancy affect those plans?*

There was silence from heaven, and we needed God's intervention badly.

36

Stumbling through the Rubble

Angie was four months pregnant. If Angie was eligible to receive WIC supplements, she could get juice, cheese, milk, eggs and other food items. All we had to do was show my proof of income, which wasn't easy, since I had no income.

I had my W-2 forms from my disability pay the previous year. Technically, there was no income to prove. This was the catch; I couldn't be the children's guardian without proving that I had the ability to take care of them. This was a sad time. It frightened me. Was I going to lose my children on top of everything else?

I prayed that God would give us favor as Angie met with the worker who was in charge of her case. They took her proof of income, with my previous year's tax return. Finally, WIC approved Angie's enrollment. WIC coupons helped put food on the table. Thank God, He was once again making a way where there was no way.

Adam complained about our poverty. He didn't like living life on a budget. He believed in God, but his faith needed to grow.

"Mom," he said, not looking me in the eye, "I…I, uh, well, I'm embarrassed that Angie's…uh…Pregnant. I've tried to be strong and believe that God would make a way somehow, but I…uh, I need more to eat—and I need an allowance."

Adam shuffled his feet and went on, "I don't want to do this, but I'm going to ask Dad if I can go live with him."

As it turned out, Mortimer told him to come, so he went. I stood and watched as my youngest son took his clothes and VCR and walked out the door.

I thought, *this is one of the saddest days of my life, to see my family splitting up.*

I knew that his father was his favorite parent, but I'd been hoping that he wouldn't leave. Now both sons were gone. It was just Angie and I, and at one point she almost went, too.

She might as well leave with Adam, I thought, *I'm not sure I can handle this teenage pregnancy and a new baby.*

However, Angie begged to stay with me, and I had to trust God to give me a new attitude.

At last, I applied for welfare. The handouts were inadequate for the family's budgets, and the church was doing what they could. They had a program where they gave away food once a month. That help came in handy, but I still needed an income.

I thought, *Maybe multilevel marketing would help.*

But I had too many physical and mental scars for that to be successful. So, I did what I had to do, I applied for welfare. I took my application and all my proofs of my possessions with me to Social Services for help. I received food stamps immediately. I was thankful we were able to feed my daughter balanced, stable meals. At least our bellies were full.

For months, I waited for the hearing date on my Worker's Compensation petition. I signed a promissory note. Once I won that case, I would pay them back. I was sure of winning.

While I waited for Social Services to approve my case, my utilities payments were in arrears, in the middle of winter. I went in to the welfare office once more. What delayed my answer? At last, they discovered that somebody forgot to send me my *denial.*

This couldn't be happening. They told me that I had a little over $19 too much income, they denied my request. I could not believe my ears.

I began to cry. "How am I going to take care of my pregnant daughter?"

The worker reached for her box of tissue.

"Please don't do this to me," I sobbed.

Another worker walked up, saying: "It's we State workers who earn just too much to get help when we need it."

They all tried to calm me down.

"Look," the worker said, "you'll have to try again and file. This time you might qualify."

I went directly to the church and spoke with Bishop Ellis. He said: "Bring your bills and take them to Trustee Hardy. We will do all we can to help.

When I told my family what happened, they too helped. Both my family and the church helped us stay afloat.

37

Tugging at the Heartstrings

Bishop David L. Ellis was like my other father. We were close, but after the shooting we were even closer. He watched out for me. I am so glad that his family shared him with me. He would periodically shake my hand, and leave money in it, not a $5 or $10 bill, but hundreds.

He would say, "Buy your family some neck bones."

Bishop's generous heart ached because of my poverty.

He told me, "Hold your head high. Don't let anybody convince you that you're not somebody."

He encouraged me, but sometimes I would frustrate him, and he'd scold me by saying, "You're too anointed to be so fearful."

He'd hurt my feelings, but I knew he was right. I just didn't know how to get out of that cycle of fear.

On March 19, 1996, Rex, my youngest brother, and I were having lunch, and Angie was at home in her last days of pregnancy. She did not feel well that day, so I left her home alone to rest. I went to lunch to get a break away from all the drama.

After lunch, my brother and I returned to his home where we found a message from Angie to call home.

"Oh, Mom," she cried when she answered the phone, *"Bishop Ellis died."*

"No." I cried, unable to believe what she'd said. "No, it isn't true. You must have it wrong."

I jumped in my car and drove to the church, sure that this was a sad joke. Bishop Ellis was bigger than life, so how could he be dead? We found that it was only too true. He was in Arkansas, at a winter conference for the Pentecostal Assemblies of the World, when he died; his family flew his body home.

The place was a bedlam of crying, weeping and mayhem. Men, women, and children were everywhere, sobbing. Our leader was gone. What were we going to do?

It finally hit me that Angie was home, in her condition, dealing with that news alone. I drove home, where Angie and I sobbed together. I had trouble accepting his death.

However, in God's wisdom, he let death take one life and birth bring in another. On March 23, 1996, Nathan David was born—without a cord around his neck.

For some time, I'd been having dreams that he was going to be still-born with the cord around his neck. My anxiety increased as I carried that burden. When born, he was fine except for one thing—he was blue. His eyes weren't open, nor was he crying. My babies screamed at birth. Nathan did not make a sound.

"Breathe, Nathan, breathe," I cried.

Oh, God, help. He isn't breathing.

It seemed like an eternity until the nurse suctioned his throat and smacked his bottom. Then he let out one yelp. He didn't have much to say, but he looked around as if to say, "Who turned the lights on?"

Handsome described Nathan. He had facial features like his mother and a fair complexion like his Dad. What a miracle! What an exhilarating experience, to see the birth of my first grandbaby.

Angie and Jeff decided to name him Nathan Antonio. However, in memory of Bishop David Ellis, Nathan's middle name changed to David. I nicknamed him "Grandma's Sunshine." I didn't care how he got into the world, he was *here*, and we were going to love him.

The doctor's diagnosed Nathan with jaundice, so they kept him at the hospital. Dr. Shea released Angie from the hospital on the day of Bishop's funeral. Nathan's liver malfunctioned, so he stayed. I could not mourn at the cemetery; instead I went to the hospital.

Members at our church had trouble accepting Bishop Ellis' death too. This pastor had been everybody's dad or friend. Only time could heal the pain from the loss. The church voted to install Charles, his oldest son, as interim pastor. Pastor Charles told the congregation, "We've been trained for such a time as this. We must hang together and we'll all get through it."

We did get through it, but Charles could not fill the void nor ease the pain. Sometimes I wondered if we made Bishop Ellis a god to us, instead of God Himself.

Nathan came home a few days later. He and I hit it off well. I had trouble holding and walking with him. I made an appointment with the orthopedic doctor who put me into physical therapy again. When the therapist asked me what motivated me to get better. I answered, "I want to be able to play with my grandson."

His birth fueled a new determination to get back all that I'd lost.

When Nathan was three months old, Angie graduated with honors from high school. When he was five months old, she left for the University of Michigan. In the years that passed, she earned two college degrees, receiving her Master of Public Health degree with honors.

Today, she and Nathan are doing just fine. He is eight and she is 25. Angie married Nathan's father as soon as she completed her undergraduate degree and Nathan was four years old. They lived together as a married couple for six months; then Nathan's father left.

On paper, their marriage lasted two years. Angie divorced, moved on, and is a lovely woman and mother.

38

Hit by Cupid's Arrows

Two years after the shooting, I was still trying to find ways to get back to some likeness of normalcy. Then, our pastor decided to develop social events for singles. He called a mass rally for us to address our concerns. It surprised the women to see new male faces.

The number of single men exceeded our expectations. One guy caught my eye, but no one knew who he was. This handsome, sturdy, stranger stood over six feet tall, with broad shoulders like a football player. He stood erect, projecting an air of confidence and an image that he could conquer the world if given a chance. I liked what I saw. I inquired to see who knew him. No one had any information about the man, except that he was single.

In a few weeks, we formed a Singles Group for divorcees, widows and widowers. We called it Single Again, and formed a board. I accepted a position on the board. We had a good core group, but needed a few more people to handle responsibilities. A few people responded to our announcement for help. The mysterious man was one of them. I found out his name, L. C. Smith, Jr.

He was single, but attached. He was in a committed friendship, and his answer disappointed me, but I was glad to have someone on the board with fresh ideas. He had good ideas to help the singles. I liked the way he thought.

He wanted us to have rules and guidelines to conduct business. He found that I was one of the few singles who wanted to act on, not just *talk* about, the subject of organization. I was willing to follow and help with the bylaws. I didn't know what we needed to do, but I was willing to learn.

He and I began talking regularly. It gave me hope that such a person existed, and maybe one day I would have a man of my own with such solid ideas.

My friends who met him felt he was just the person for me, however, that was not possible.

One day, the singles' board met at my house. Just before this, I had all my plumbing replaced, only to create a new problem. The plumber only fixed the pipes, but left *holes*. Since I had limited money, I was at the mercy of those who could help me.

People promised to come and fix them, but never came nor called. So, during the meeting I mentioned my problem, and this new man volunteered right away to help. He promised to work on the project for two hours the next day, which was a Saturday.

He didn't know me well, but said, "The brothers should look out for their single sisters as if they were blood sisters. I'm from Alabama, and they taught men to care for the women."

Can you believe he came Saturday as he had promised, and fixed the holes? I was so happy to get help. He and my father got along well, and I liked him, too. From that day on, we became friends. I became his confidant about a friendship with his girlfriend, Victoria, and he became mine. I had made some poor decisions about men, and talking to him helped me with my loneliness.

After some time I asked, "Can you define your friendship with Victoria? Are you committed to her? You must not be spending much time with her, because *we're* always talking."

He must have thought about it, because eventually they broke up and he and I started dating.

At that point I thought God smiled on me. L. C. worked at General Motors for GMAC, and was going to school to get his Bachelors of Business Administration degree. In addition, L. C. was taking care of his mother, with whom he shared an apartment. This was one cool dude.

Could I have found the man for whom I was looking? It had been two years since the divorce and shooting, so surely that was enough time to get my head together. Although I was still periodically suffering from depression, it disappeared when we talked.

Somehow, I got the impression that he proposed marriage. How had we gone in one night from dating to being fiancées? Obviously, I didn't understand his plans. He wasn't proposing marriage but sex. He didn't try to correct me, either. As a Christian, I assumed he believed like me, no sex before marriage. So I thought he wanted to marry me. I told everyone about our impending nuptials.

I don't know why he never stopped me. He even told his mother, and made plans for her to move in with us when we married eight months later. We made plans to blend our families together.

We delayed our marriage plans for eight months so he could complete his undergraduate degree. My teenagers and physical therapy kept me busy. I noticed that the strain of working and going to college had my new beau wound up like a spinning top, ready for launching. We had dated only a month and a half when our first major crisis occurred. On December 17, 1994, his mother developed a blood clot that almost killed her. On that day, we had planned to pick out my engagement ring, but instead we spent the day in the hospital.

During his mother's recovery that followed, it seemed there was never time to get my ring. I don't know what happened between us, but eventually, in June of 1995 we broke up. This was just before he graduated from the Detroit College of Business with a Bachelors Degree in Business Administration. I must say, I was still proud of his accomplishment, even though we were no longer a couple. To go back to school at 40 and compete with young, sharp minds took determination and vision. It wasn't easy to overcome obstacles, gain the prize, and prepare for a brighter future.

39

Back from Sanity's Edge

While I was focusing on my loss, God was trying to get me to look beyond it and toward a plan that He had for my future.

John 12:24 states; *Verily, verily, I say unto you, Except a corn of wheat fall into the ground and die, it abideth alone: but if it die, it bringeth forth much fruit.*

He wanted me to see a brighter future with a greater purpose. One event after another was destroying the life that I built. I mourned to see all my hard work go down the tubes. Marriage gone. Youth gone. Career gone. Pastor died. Spiritual career gone. Children gone.

All the people and places that I depended on crumbled under the weight of trouble. I had no more crutches or old supports. All the devastation brought me to the feet of Jesus to ask for some answers. In my best moments, I would cry out and declare that I needed God more than ever. I don't want to even think about my worst moments.

In Mark 2:17, Jesus said; *They that are whole have no need of the physician, but they that are sick....*

I needed a physician for my spiritual maladies. I needed Jesus to heal my broken spirit.

Paul said in Romans 8:26;

"Likewise the Spirit also helpeth our infirmities: for we know not what we should pray for as we ought; but the Spirit itself maketh intercession for us with groanings which cannot be uttered.

That promise reassured me that I had all the help I needed, if I would allow the Holy Spirit to pray on my behalf.

At last, as I used my prayer language, a peace and calmness emerged. I was able to take baby steps toward change. An inner applause thundered after each victory. Hope in God was surfacing. If I were to recover, I was going to have to get in the game and I needed tools to perform that.

First, I continued my daily prayer life and Bible study. It was hard to retain what I read, so I wrote down most of my studies and kept a daily log. I wrote letters to God daily, and jotted down His answers so I would remember His solutions.

Second, I needed to settle the issue of the shooting with God. Why didn't he protect me? I wanted an answer.

He answered, *"You were heading down a path of self-destruction. I allowed the shooting to take place to distract you from suicide. You had a broken heart, and lost your need to live."*

I forgot—while I was in the hospital, God did tell me that. He had said, *You have a choice to live or die. If you choose to live, you will have to fight to get back on your feet. But, if your will is to die, then I will let you die honorably. Everyone will say that you died of the injuries from the shooting, but you would have died of a broken heart. You are in covenant with me, and I have attached My name to yours. If you choose death, it must be honorable, not through the disgrace of suicide.*

In the end, I chose life. I needed a starting point. So, I began reading self-help books, biographies and memoirs. The testimonies gave me the courage to hold onto to my faith. I reestablished my faith in God and searched out more and more folks who had faced adversity—and won. I read book after book about overcomers.

In the book, *Girl Interrupted,* by Susanna Kaysen, she described her teenage confinement in a mental hospital. It was there that she found herself.

She was in transition from a teenager to young adult. Susanna did not have enough coping tools. This lack led to a mental health confinement. During the confinement, she was able to gain clarity and start her journey back to wholeness.

In the book, *A Beautiful Mind,* Slyvia Nasar described Dr. Nash's confinements for mental illness. He had to believe *past* the illness to free the genius inside him. He struggled and used many means to overcome his illness, and he didn't quit.

In Cheryl Bass Foster's memoir, *Broken to be Made Whole,* she wanted to die. Her broken life crushed her will to live. Once she experienced a meeting with God, He changed her broken life of failure into success.

Frank McCourt wrote, *Angela's Ashes.* In his memoir, he detailed his impoverished childhood. Poverty almost devoured his poor Irish family. Trouble found them, no matter how hard they tried to overcome it.

He learned, from his father that drinking to cover the pain didn't work. Frank made different choices than his father. He grabbed opportunities to better himself. He went from a sickly boy to a schoolteacher—and then to a best-selling author. Yes. He turned out all right.

These are just a sampling of the books I read that encouraged me, to try, until my life turned around. It took action on my part to achieve that dream. James 2:20 says:...*Faith without works is dead.*

I also studied heroes in the Bible who overcame extreme odds. I noticed that all of these people had a vision of their future before they could adequately execute their plan of action. Job, Joseph, and Mephibosheth all were Biblical overcomers.

Job suffered a total reversal in his prosperity, posterity, health, marriage, and community influence. He was in agony, but he never gave up. At the end of the book of Job, the Bible says, *"So the Lord blessed the latter end of Job more than his beginning...."*

Joseph was a young Hebrew boy, born to Jacob. Jacob was the patriarch of a large, wealthy family. Joseph, the eleventh of twelve sons, found favor with his father but drew hatred from his brothers. Jacob gave Joseph a coat of many colors; it made his brothers jealous. The jealousy turned to rage and they sold him into slavery. For thirty years, this act of jealousy separated him from his family.

In his young life, Joseph went from slavery to prison, and then from prison to Pharaoh's assistant, second in command in the land of Egypt. Yes. His end was better than his beginning.

Mephibosheth, King Saul's grandson, was a baby when an enemy killed the royal family. As the royal family was running for their lives, his nurse, who was his caretaker, dropped him. This fall left him with crippled feet, disabled for life.

He hid in obscurity until his adulthood and then King David remembered a promise he made to his friend, Jonathan, Mephibosheth's father. David promised that he would look after his seed.

King David took Mephibosheth from poverty to the palace where he regained his royal rights and privileges. He ate at the King's table continually. Yes. He went from riches to rags—and back to riches.

What was the common thread that bound them all together? Their trust and faith in God was their commonality.

Yes. I would do well to remember that.

40

Cutting through Red Tape

I was determined to get better. I knew the key to getting better was to build my faith and trust God more. It seemed to get harder to do that when emotional pains and hurts just kept coming. I needed more courage to keep fighting in court to win money that I qualified to receive. I just needed to convince the courts that I was entitled to it.

There was no let-up in pressure. Bishop Ellis was buried on a Monday and the Worker's Compensation trial was held two days later.

At the opening in the hearing I fell apart. I cried when they asked my name, education, and employment history. The magistrate took a recess giving me a chance to compose myself. Recounting my employment history was hard for me.

When I started with the State of Michigan at 21, I wanted to make a difference in people's lives. I was young and eager to help people turn their lives around, but at the trial I was a long way from that goal. I felt like a has-been asking for a hand out.

My employer had promised that if injured on-the-job I would have Worker's Compensation as a stopgap measure. I now needed that help and no one wanted to give it to me. The only way to get help was to fight.

It was brutal. The assistant attorney general, Denita Vancourt, kept hammering at my character, but she was unable to find anything. I did my job and took pride in a job well done. I never thought that I would have to defend myself against my employer.

The only other witness at the trial, besides myself, was my former supervisor, Countessa Cortland. Denita asked her if she knew me. She affirmed it. When asked about my character she said, "Denise was the most honest person in the Department."

"Ms. Cortland, How long have you known her?"

"About 20 years."

"Would you lie for her?"

"No, I am a Christian. I don't lie for anyone."

"Do you remember June 11, 1993?"

"No, I will have to refer to the report. If the report has my signature on it, then it is true to the best of my knowledge."

This was the witness against me. Both sides had summoned her as a witness.

The judge, Madeline Murphy, saw that the assistant attorney general, Denita Vancourt, was intimidating me, so she took over and began asking me questions.

She could not understand why I felt that I was unsafe at work. Why did I believe the anonymous caller? Once she was able to prove there was a call, she told me that she was going to rule in my favor.

"Ms. Thomason, tell me about the safe keeping of Violation of Probation files," Judge Murphy asked.

"After the judge signs a violation of probation warrant, they place it in a safe location until the arraignment on the warrant. It guarantees the information will be available at the Violation of Probation hearing. In this case, the file had disappeared. No one could find the file that proved why I revoked his probation."

"So this made you afraid?"

"Yes. A friend, who was a supervisor, was trying to find it for me. Her boss told her that if she found it she was to make a copy of the file and then hide it. After they looked everywhere they thought possible, she called me and said: "We can't find the file.""

"The anonymous caller said that this man bought his way out of his violation, and his whole file disappeared. Within 30 days after returning to work, a second shooting occurred. I could no longer feel safe, nor did I trust anyone. I went home."

At last, after much deliberation, the judge weighed the evidence and found in favor of me. I lost on one count, for the disability on my right knee.

When I smashed both knees in August 1992, I had severely hurt the left knee. I had to report both knees in case they gave me trouble later. They did. The court said that we failed to present enough documentation for the right knee. However, I won the psychological damage. The left knee improved with physical therapy, so it was better. I won. I had an income.

However, I didn't receive a check until July. The payment the judge quoted was in error. I called my attorney, who agreed to adjust the amount I received without going to the Appeals Court. With much prayer, my case never reached the Appeals Court. Thank God for another supernatural intervention.

My story about disability didn't end at the trial. Aetna Disability commanded me to apply for Social Security. After six months or more on disability, a client had to apply for Social Security Disability. Aetna stopped payment if the claimant didn't file.

If eligible and accepted, the client then had to pay back all the money Aetna paid for disability. Failure to apply would close the claim.

I lost on the first application, so I appealed and lost again. I then asked for a trial, which took place in July 1996. Aetna recommended me to a company called Disability Services, which represented me in the trial.

One of the toughest magistrates presided over my hearing. In fear and trembling, I went to trial. When I entered the courtroom, the judge apologized for making me come. He reassured me that the trial was going to be brief and that he was going to rule in my favor, but said he needed to ask a few questions for the record. Often, he inquired to my comfort, and then he let me go.

It happened so fast that it stunned my representative. He said, "Do you realize what just happened? You won."

Then he asked, "Did you see the report that your psychiatrist wrote?"

"No, I didn't."

"Well, it told what you went through and how the strain of all of it was pushing you to thoughts of suicide."

I looked at him in astonishment. What a break. This was a miracle, thank God.

When the settlement finally came, I paid back Aetna over $66,000, and I took a much-needed rest, and went to Arizona for two weeks.

During that time, I did almost nothing but visit with relatives and make a new start. We saw the "Wild, Wild West," visiting Tombstone Territory, the O.K. Corral, the Crystal Saloon, Boot Hill, and other landmarks.

I was surprised to learn that the Buffalo Soldiers were black. Oh, thank God He allowed me to take that trip, because He knew that I was going to need that break. All hell broke loose on my return. But by God's grace, He managed to turn evil into good on my behalf.

My old friend, Barry, met me at the airport to drive me home. The first bombshell landed while we were driving down I-94. He said, "Denise, I am engaged."

Oh, God, not that. I thought, terrified that he was going to bring that up again. *I can't marry him, Lord, and that's that.*

"Denise...I, uh," he said clearing his throat. "You've been a good friend to me for a long time. Now...I'm not sure how to say this, but you've taught me what a woman ought to be—and the man she likes. What I need to be to gain a *good* wife. So, what I want you to know is—I've found that woman and we're getting married in October."

Sagging in my seat, I thought, *That took me by surprise. I sure didn't see that one coming—but Oh, God. Thanks. He's marrying somebody else.*

No sooner had Barry driven away than Mortimer made a surprise visit to my home. He got out of his car and came up the walk, his head down. I waited for him on the porch, holding onto the railing. He said nothing until he reached the steps, stopped, looked up at me and said, "Denise, I need to talk with you. You got time?"

Okay. I thought. *What's up now? Mortimer doesn't just drop in for a friendly chitchat.*

As it turned out, he could no longer care for Adam. The upshot of this was that Adam was coming home—my son was coming home to me.

Oh, thank You, Jesus.

41

Spiritual Recovery

When I woke up in the recovery room after my surgery from the shooting, I found tubes attached all over my body. These tubes were there to sustain my life while my body healed. After a while, I didn't need as many tubes to pump in lifesaving fluids. Eventually, the day came when I was tube-free.

Recovering emotionally was similar. I had developed some bad habits that I needed to shed, like fear, anxiety, anger, and self-pity, to mention a few. These attachments were different than the life saving tubes, and increased after I left the hospital. While at first they seemed to keep me safe, I found that all they did was create a prison from which it was difficult to escape.

At the Day Hospital they taught us tools so we could let go of the attachments that mainly serve to tie us down and hold us back. My intellect understood, but my emotions still wanted to hide. The principles taught in the book, *SOS: Help for Emotions*, written by Lynn Clark, Ph.D., reminded me of my daily seminars at the hospital.

Irrational Beliefs was my favorite. How do you convince irrational people that their thoughts are not rational? Try living a day through my eyes. I didn't feel safe. I didn't make up the shooting or my injuries. I had the scars to show for proof. Surely I lived in reality. I needed someone to explain to me my irrational beliefs. How was anyone going to prove to me that what I felt was not real?

Anger, how could someone explain to me why I should not be angry? I believed that anger was a proper attitude in such a situation.

Why should I let it go? If I let it go, I was afraid I couldn't fight for a normal life again.

Depression is frozen anger. I wanted the shooter, and the man who had me shot, to feel the same pain that I'd had. I was afraid to let the lid off all that pent-up anger, so I let it weigh my spirit down with sadness and self-pity. Anyone who tried to show me the bright side met my resistance.

I didn't want anyone quoting scriptures about turning the other cheek. And I didn't want to *forgive*.

Elder Graham, a minister at the church, sat me down one day and said, "Now, daughter, you are going to have to forgive that man."

Humph, I thought. *He can quote all the scriptures he wants, but right now forgiveness is not on the menu.*

This bad attitude went on and on. Years passed and I still needed healing. I prayed, read my Bible and went to church but still could not find deliverance. The unforgiveness ate at my heart. The words from the Bible were empty. I refused to admit that Elder Graham gave me good counsel and the secret to my healing was in *obedience* to the Word, not merely in hearing it.

Proverbs 24:16: *For a just man falleth seven times, and riseth up again: but the wicked shall fall into mischief.*

It is the truth from this passage of scripture that I have lived, bad attitude and all. God knew the contrary attitude was temporary. I had gained it as my reaction to what I couldn't understand, but it wasn't who I was in my heart.

God knew how to take my broken soul and restore it to health. No matter what happened, God, had the ability to raise me up from the ash heap of despair. I never stopped believing that I could rise again.

David found restoration. He tells the story in Psalms 23:1 "*The Lord is my shepherd. I shall not want.*"

He saw God as the shepherd of his life. God met his needs. He did not need to worry because God had everything under control. He learned through his friendship with God that he could trust Him to take care of all his affairs. I needed to trust God.

42

Bursting the Cocoon of Darkness

Craziness is repeating the same mistakes in the same way and expecting improved results. For the first few years of my journey back to health I did just that, and stayed in the prison of depression.

When I tried, and choices didn't turn out the way I had hoped, I supported my own worthlessness and didn't try again for a while. When no rescuer came to deliver me, I realized that if it were going to be it was up to me to seek help.

Sanity, I learned, is trying different methods to achieve a successful result, such as refueling my dreams, getting rid of old ways, and finding healthier ways to handle problems. One way I handled my problems was called critical thinking. I learned if I asked the right questions to solve a problem and found the right answers, I could bring about a change in my life. Questions like: Am I in a rut? Are my goals reasonable? Am I setting myself up for failure? These answers brought about truths that set me free, one step at a time.

I had to take a fresh, new direction. Dream again. I had to see myself as I would be in six months, one year, five years, even ten. What was I doing to achieve this goal? What would it require?

I made plans, set time increments and dates for completion of those plans. I tried to stay on track, but couldn't. I had to learn to be flexible and adjust the plan when the new me didn't respond as quick as I wanted to, but I didn't give up. Change was necessary. The new plan had achievable goals. I learned to crawl before I could walk. Baby steps were frustrating. In real life, saying, "Just do it" doesn't always work.

The adage "If at first you don't succeed try, try again" was good advice for me to follow. I inhaled the information contained in those biographies of people who became successful even after some serious failures. It became clear that only the person who looks at failure as an *opportunity to learn* would reach his or her dream.

I already mentioned Job, Joseph, Mephibosheth and others who had faith to believe that circumstances were going to change. They looked ahead in time and believed God would step into their circumstances. What they were doing today was going to make a difference for tomorrow.

At any point, if they had not held onto their faith in God they would have died in defeat. Instead they trusted that He was working His plans out in their lives. They made the best of hardships and lived to see a change in their circumstances.

My obstructed vision sometimes diverted my attention away from God. During these moments I had some challenges. I learned that sometimes He allowed a little trouble to burn up the obstacles to help me to get back on track. He will not allow me to stray too far. He invested too much in me to leave me stranded on the highways of life. He sent help through unusual methods, some of which I welcomed, and some not. I have admitted many times that His ways were not mine, and mine were not His (Isaiah 55:8-9). I couldn't believe that God failed to protect me from the murderer. He allowed it, and we didn't always see eye-to-eye.

One day God called me by my name in prayer.

Denise, there is no denying that these events happened to you. I just don't interpret them the same way you do.

"God, then how do you see it?"

As an act of love.

"Love."

Yes, love. When I refuse to let you stay stuck in a cycle of defeat that is love.

"God, that is a strange way to show Your love."

You think it is all right to just survive.

"God, I don't understand."

A vicious cycle to please began when you married Mortimer. He was a good person to befriend, but as a spouse it was a mismatch from the beginning.

"Well. Yeah."

The hole in the marriage kept getting bigger and bigger and you tried harder and harder to repair it.

"True."

See, Denise, all you were doing was wearing out before your time.

"God, you are telling the truth."

You neglected all your talents because you were on the wrong track with the need to please.

"God, I think I see what You are saying."

Oh, it didn't stop there. You let this behavior spill into other areas of your life and it became your motto, 'I aim to please.'

"God, I knew no other way to have a relationship. I guess I felt that it was the only way to get people to like me."

Don't please man, Denise, but please Me. Seek first My kingdom and all its virtue and the rest I will give to you.

"Now, God, it is easier to talk about it than it is to perform. I want to please You, but sometimes I detour."

I will give you healthier friendships that will encourage dependence on Me. I will re-route your path in such a way that pleasing man will drop out of sight and pleasing Me will remain.

What I didn't understand was God's plan for maturity. If you want to grow in Him, settle it right now, you are going to go through fiery tests and trials. That's God's way.

The fire purges anything in your way that impedes your growth. My God-inspired plans survived the fire, but those that I did "in the name of the Lord," but He did author, burned up (1 Cor. 3:10-15). He wants to show us off as His obedient and loving children. Sometimes I needed an attitude adjustment to keep that harmonious relationship with Him. I didn't understand that, *whom God loves, He chastens.* Fire is a great attitude adjuster.

I had to learn that what you say to yourself—self-talk—makes or breaks recovery. The enemies to positive change are anger, self-pity, blame/shame, bitterness, depression, unforgiveness and fear. They all are opponents to change. If they are not addressed, they will erode your life and destroy any possibility for positive change. I had to learn it the hard way.

While I was in the Day Hospital, they held seminars about topics that would help us to heal. Anger was such a topic. Webster's definition of anger is, "...a strong feeling of displeasure and antagonism. Anger, the most general term, names the reaction, but in itself tells nothing about the intensity or justification...of the emotional state..." (Webster, 1996) p. 157

I learned that *I* was causing my anger. My self-talk set up the responding behavior. The result was aggressive, angry behavior. I thought this was acceptable.

It was hard, initially, to believe that my anger was unhealthy. I held unforgiveness toward my employer who transferred me to the high-risk unit. It angered me that no one debriefed me about the shooting. My superiors acted as if they did not recognize it as job-related. I felt abandoned, and angry.

Before entering the Day Hospital, I wanted revenge, and someone was going to have to pay. Learning how to diffuse anger is important.

First, I examined who or what triggered these emotions. Then, I considered what control I had over the circumstances and which ones were out of my hands. When I learned which ones I could control, I felt better and learned to choose proper responses.

I had to learn that I had the power to turn anger on, as well as turn it off. No one makes me angry. I choose the reaction. If I choose it, then I must take responsibility for the results of the choice.

Self-pity was my favorite. It seemed so noble and righteous, but it was harder to understand. I found I was just rehearsing what happened and all the reasons I was a victim.

Was I not justified in saying, "No one understands where I've been and what's happened? Isolation from the public made sense to me. People were just too insensitive to feel my pain.

I had to learn that self-pity is a deceptive emotion. It presents itself as empathetic or sympathetic, but in reality it's the jailer to a self-made prison.

As long as I told myself that I'm a victim, the longer I would stay in the dark prison of self-pity. I had to learn to mother myself and say congratulatory words when I stepped out of the darkness to peek at the light. I took leaves of absence from the dark cell, which now has a sign that says, open for occupancy. I am not living there any more.

Some days I forget that I have moved, and God has to remind me.

Denise, I love you everyday of your life, so you do not have to return to bad habits. You don't have to seek love in the wrong places any more. Self-pity is not your home, leave it vacant.

"God, it is a habit that I need to break."

If you will rest in Me, My love will break the cycle. It will bring you joy, purpose and satisfaction. Your hungry soul will not need food, pleasing or any other compulsion to try to satisfy the hunger.

"I just want that inner gnawing to go away. It is like I am hungry all the time even when I am full."

You describe the hunger of your soul. You eat and eat, gaining more weight, yet the gnawing continues. Physically, it caused you to be overweight, but spiritually it causes leanness to the soul or, simply stated, immaturity.

"I understand that. No matter how many diets I begin, it never brings about a permanent solution."

My child, it is not a food problem; it is a spiritual one. You tried so hard to please everyone that you buried the real you. I will help you to find your buried treasure. The one I created has a purpose different from the life that you have led.

"Wow, that's deep."

Seek me day and night through prayer, meditation and reading the word. I will reveal the plan and get you back on track. Helping people is your passion. Let me show you how to do it My way.

Each day God has shown me some assessment of my spiritual progress. Like a proud father, He watches me explore new challenges. I believe that sometimes He laughs and sometimes He is sad when He sees me struggling to understand life. Sometimes I stop maturing. God knows exactly what I need to get me back on track—and He'll do the same for you.

43

Battered Beliefs

I needed to learn how to live a victorious spiritual life. Too many times I let Satan appeal to my logic and I ended up in trouble. Logic and spiritual things do not mix. When I let my mind, will, emotions, logic and feelings make a carnal decision, it does not please God.

But the natural man receiveth not the things of the Spirit of God: for they are foolishness unto him, neither can he know them, because they are spiritually discerned. (I Corinthians 2:14)

Spiritual matters are not governed by logic. My pride deceived me into believing I was okay. Only the Spirit of God saw beneath the surface and knew my true motives. Self-loathing was about to kill, steal and destroy my future.

First, my confidence in God and my image of being His child was being challenged. When that didn't succeed, then suicidal thoughts bombarded my mind. Yes, I felt the torment but I could not let them win. I couldn't let anything destroy my faith in God.

Remember, Isaiah 54:17 says that *No weapon formed against you will prosper....* Satan can form the weapon of destruction and the strategy to carry it out, but the intent behind the weapon will not succeed.

That's what happened to me. The original contract for hire was to kill me. When that didn't happen, then he activated Plan 2. Deception's job was to convince me that I did something wrong to bring on such violence. When that didn't work, Satan began Plan 3. Self-pity's job was to convince me that God didn't love me—or if He did, why didn't He protect me? Plan 4 set me up for death when I didn't fall for none of the other lies. Then Satan pushed harder, introducing the thought of suicide.

After losing my husband to divorce and losing my ability to perform my job as a probation officer, I was feeling purposeless. Satan worked in my mind to try to convince me that life wasn't worth living—but God had put wonderful people around me. Over and again, my children expressed their thanks that God let me live. They still needed my love and guidance. My parents and siblings were busy trying to handle their own affairs, but they showed love in unique ways. Three siblings were having severe marriage problems, but they stopped the feuds and focused on my healing, forming a chain of protection around me.

Then there were the friends that God assigned to my psychological well being. They gave me freedom to call any time of the day or night. They didn't just give lip service but walked with me so I could stay on this side of sanity. They'd listen to the strange thought patterns without judging me. They made sure that I knew how precious I was to them, reminding me how many times I'd done the same, year-in and year-out, for them.

They helped by telling me who I was and about how many people were better because I lived. They fed me positive affirmations, which raised my self-esteem a notch or two, and kept me from suicide. They spoon-fed me self-worth and the Word of God.

We created our own phrases: *I can't see real well out of my eyes, so I will use your eyes to help me see better.*

Or, when they were battling with me, they'd say, *I have my own eyes and I don't see through your damaged eyes. I see a vibrant woman who is temporarily struggling, not a struggling woman who had only temporary victories in the past.*

They refused to let me go to that dark hole of depression alone. If I went in so did they, and in so doing they loved me back to a stable place.

My psychiatrist helped too. He never let on that I was as messed up as I was. He'd let me tell him what I was thinking, and he'd replace the garbage with healthier information. It was a hard task, because my memory was damaged. I could not retain information.

He had to tell it to me over and again. He questioned me to see if I was changing or even understood. He had to deal with days when I felt betrayed by his actions, I saw him as an enemy. He had to teach me that we could have a difference of opinion but it was not betrayal. That idea was hard to grasp. I saw life as either black or white. You were either with me or against me. He was patient and determined to shift my way of thinking.

44

Boomerang

L. C. and I ended our relationship on a sour note, so I didn't want to talk to him. He tried to be friends, but I wanted no part of it. He was gone and good riddance. I was moving on.

We had no further contact for a year and a half until his mother died in August of 1996, and he left a message on my answering machine to let me know that she died. I was out of town at the time, but when I got the message, it surprised me. He thought enough of me to call, and inform me that a wonderful mother and spiritual warrior had died.

We eventually stopped playing phone tag and had a good talk. It was good hearing from him. A few months went by, and a new Spike Lee Joint movie came out called *Get on the Bus*.

Somehow this movie triggered a need for me to want to talk to L. C. and clean up unfinished business. Part of this involved forgiveness—oh, yes, forgiveness, and I still didn't like that word—but our new friendship began well.

I enjoyed this man, and I believe he enjoyed me, too. In November 1996, I took him out for his birthday. I picked him up and took him to dinner, where he was "king for a day."

Then in January, 1997, I needed an escort for dinner. He took me, dressed in his tuxedo, looking dapper. He was such a gentleman. One month later, on my birthday, he asked me to marry him. This time, I did not misinterpret it. He wrote it in my birthday card. He wanted me to be his wife—he did.

Four months later, on May 3, 1997, we married in a private ceremony at my house in front of 25 family and friends. Bishop Charles Ellis III performed the wedding. Wonder of wonders, L. C. took me to the Bahamas for a weeklong honeymoon in his time-share.

Oh, God, I thought, *You're giving me back double joy for all my troubles.*

Such joy. What a wonderful man.

For one, I liked my new husband because he was a dreamer. He thought big and had lofty plans and goals. L. C. fascinated me by his diction and his descriptive words. He saw the world as a place for opportunities. He always had some new plan he was achieving, which he seemed confident would change his life and make him rich.

L. C. also had a unique friendship with God. He called Him "Daddy" and prayed to Him the same way, receiving unique results. I liked that. L. C. wasn't stuffy like some of my church friends. Often, most of us were so self-assured and superior to sinners that we were unapproachable. L. C. was down-to-earth in his conversation. It was an exciting time to begin a new marriage with a new attitude.

In my new life, I met people free and not bound by my fear. They didn't know my baggage, so they didn't treat me as a fragile egg. They saw my potential and pushed me ahead. My husband was one of those people. He was my personal cheerleader, but sometimes he was downright irritating. He didn't make it *comfortable* for me to waste the rest of my life.

If I was going to feel sorry for myself then I was going to do it with him nagging me all the way. It was up to me. I could hang back, or forge ahead with God. It was that simple.

L. C. was a computer analyst, and he kept analyzing me to see where I needed to change. Discipline and order always were difficult for me (still are); so he created a program on our computer to help me remember the names of people I met. From there he branched out and sat me down to learn how to use the computer's many tools.

I didn't know it then, but that computer was to be the bridge to my new life, even though at first I learned to use it just to keep L. C. at bay. Finally, as I grew more familiar with it, I began to realize that L. C. was right—this was a valuable tool.

"Baby, you have so much potential but fear has you bound."

"I know, but I am doing the best I can."

"I am not mad at you but at the devil, because he has robbed your potential."

"Why do you say that?"

"Denise, he convinced you that you are ineffective; never to rise again."

"It's not the devil, L. C. it is just the way it is."

"See, that's what I am talking about. Don't resign yourself to live in a world of fear. I tell you what, I am going to pray for your total recovery."

"Thanks, Honey."

"Father, in the name of Jesus, I didn't know Denise before, but I do now. It is my duty to protect her even if it is from herself. Please shine the light of Your word on her heart. I will not sit back and see her waste away. I pray that You make the darkness light and the crooked straight so she can see how to fight."

I thought I was doing fine until he prayed. Afterwards I realized I needed Divine intervention.

45

Picking Up Shattered Pieces

About the age of four, I learned to pray. It helped me cope when faced with hard times. The spirit of fear had tormented me for most of my life. I used prayer against it. My new husband saw that fear had me bound. He knew I needed a miracle to break that stronghold in my life. But in prayer, God reassured me that he would show me the way to overcome it.

When God taught me a lesson, he used the Bible to clarify His point. One day, while doing my daily meditation, He led me to Proverbs 24:16, which states: *For a just man falleth seven times, and riseth up again: but the wicked shall fall into mischief.*

God said, *"Denise, don't let fear torment you, it will make you feel ashamed. The shame comes when you do nothing about it. You will fight many attacks against your spiritual life. This is not uncommon. Each time I will deliver you from the problem. There is no sin in having trouble. The sin is when you choose to remain in it and fail to seek My help to get out."*

"God," I said, "is that what I am doing? Accepting the problem and not seeking You to deliver me from evil?"

Yes, you decided that this was too hard for Me, so you will just have to be a fearful person. I did not give you the spirit of fear.

"So, God, what do you suggest I do to get out of the mess I am in? The shooting wasn't my idea. Yet, I became a victim. Now, You are saying that I am guilty of sin because I won't seek You for a way out."

"That is exactly what I am saying. You have a right to become whole, yet you act like a victim who has no Savior. Shake yourself and remember

that I sent my Son to die for all your sins, including this one. Turn to Psalms 23 and read verse one."

"God, it says, The Lord is my shepherd, I shall not want."

Denise, who is speaking?

"David."

"Correct."

"Who was he calling his shepherd?"

"Me".

"What does it mean?"

"That he saw Me as the shepherd and him as the sheep."

"Denise, what does a shepherd do?"

"He takes care of the sheep and attends to all their needs."

"Good. What are some of their needs?"

"Food, shelter, and protection from the wolves."

"So anything that they need, the shepherd will make it available to them?"

"Yes."

"Denise, do you see Me as your shepherd?"

"Yes."

"Really?"

"Yes, Lord, I trust you to take care of me."

"Then why won't you trust Me to heal you of the fear?"

"I don't really know. I thought I was trusting You until now."

"I want you to succeed in every part of your life. If you are afraid you won't enjoy the life that I planned for you".

"So what should I do?"

"I want you to re-read Psalms 23 and make it a part of your life. Believe like David that I am your shepherd, and anything you need I have. If you lack courage, then I can supply it. You do not have to be afraid."

This made me think. Was I causing my own immaturity through being fearful? I needed God more than ever before. So if the Lord is my shepherd and I believe it, then He meets my needs. God is not the problem. I needed to find a way to let Him change me from victim to victor.

I did as He said. I re-read Psalms 23.

The Lord is my shepherd; I shall not want. He maketh me to lie down in green pastures: He leadeth me beside the still waters. He restoreth my soul: He leadeth me in the paths of righteousness for His name's sake.

Yea, though I walk through the valley of the shadow of death, I will fear no evil: for thou art with me; thy rod and thy staff they comfort me. Thou preparest a table before me in the presence of mine enemies: thou anointest my head with oil; my cup runneth over. Surely goodness and mercy shall follow me all the days of my life: and I will dwell in the house of the Lord forever.

After reading that Psalm, I realized more of what David was saying about God. He enjoyed a friendship with God that was similar to that of sheep to a shepherd. He relied on God for everything. He learned that through the storms of life, God took care of him like the shepherd did for the sheep.

God always found a way to lead him to places of rest and renewal, to free him from hurt, harm, and danger. God made sure that he supplied him with everything he needed. David's rest from the storms of life lasted until God felt he was healthy in spirit, soul and body. His Shepherd made sure that no enemy could harm him during his restoration.

Only when David completed his renewal did he engage again in the battles of life. God protected him from destruction. David's enemies learned lessons about God, too. They could not defeat David. They realized David served a powerful God.

At the end of this Psalm, David made a vow to worship and to serve God, all the days of his life. His enemies realized that serving God brought about favorable results. David decided that he wasn't going to give his loyalty to any one else but God. He gave his heart to the only true God of Israel.

Wow, I missed a lot when I chose to live in fear. I decided to tell God all about it in prayer.

"Father, in the name of Jesus, I come to you feeling stupid. I spent all these years living in fear and I didn't have to. First, I ask you to forgive me for my ignorance. Second, I want to change my ways. Please show me how to live a victorious life and not one as a victim. Amen."

46

Life's Relay Race

An old African proverb says: "*It takes a village to raise a child.*"

For my family to get through the storms, especially during their teenage years, we needed the village. With God's help they survived, and became outstanding adults.

Aaron finished his college education. He earned his Bachelors of Science in Business Administration, from Valparaiso University. He obtained gainful employment with a local telecommunications firm. Also, he sings professionally with Chris Jones and Word of Praise. He reflects his love for God in all his endeavors. He also mentors young men to live godly.

Angela, as stated before, has completed both her undergraduate and graduate degrees from the University of Michigan. She works at the University of Michigan Hospital. She has the privilege to work, for a renowned gynecologist, as his project assistant. Through his urging, she plans to enter a doctoral program in the fall of 2005. She reflects her love for God through mentoring young women and especially teenagers. She openly speaks about her teenage pregnancy and how it changed her life.

Adam has been my long-distance child. He graduated from Savannah Arts and Design College. He earned a Bachelor of Fine Arts, in fashion design. He is an artist just like his dad.

Upon graduation, he moved to Texas. Currently he is an assistant coach for a Christian school in Texas. Also, he is enrolled in a pre-seminary program with Tom Nelson's ministries. He still is searching for balance between his love for God and fashion design.

Nathan, grandma's sunshine, basks in the fact that he is my only grandson and a thriving eight-year-old. He does well in school and plays on a basketball team at the local YMCA. God allowed me to see them all grow up. My children needed help to mature and so did I.

I believe that *"It takes a village to restore a wounded soul."* Without my good support systems, I would still be wandering. I made a career out of getting better.

Dr. Martin, at the Bio Life Health Center, told me that I needed colonics to remove all the lead the bullets deposited in my body. I also needed to clean my body from toxins. He guaranteed me that with regular colonics my energy would be restored.

So I had colonics and I did feel better, but my energy level didn't rise.

In 1995, I needed to boost my self-esteem. My friend, Venus Thues, invited me to a Mary Kay Cosmetics meeting. I needed that energy charged atmosphere that night. Disability left me feeling very disconnected. Crisette Ellis, Elder Charles Ellis' wife, led the excitement that night. I had to be a part of that group. They gave God credit for their success and they *were* making money. I didn't necessarily want to sell the cosmetics but I wanted to join women who were making positive changes in their lives. I connected with these ladies. Today, Crisette Ellis is a Senior National Sales Director in Mary Kay Cosmetics. Her charisma and friendship are still part of my life.

Then I found I had to eat right, so I discovered another program for nutrition called *Garden Ministries*. Nancy Rigsby is the minister of health and founder who introduced me to the *Hallelujah Diet* created by George Malkmus. He wrote the book *Why Christians Get Sick,* which taught me a healthier way of eating.

Malkmus was a promoter of juicing raw fruits and vegetables, and he taught that any illness or injury could be reversed with proper diet. This exciting journey included drinking vegetable and fruit juices, eating barley green supplements, flaxseeds for roughage, rice milk, and other delicious meals. Little by little I found that it was true. Diet does effect your health.

Another instructor, Cindy Pena, taught that improving my lymphatic system would improve my ability to resist colds. A fun and easy way to do this was to jump on a rebounder. It's a small trampoline, and a two-minute work out daily helps to boost the entire immune system. It did just that. This was another stepping-stone on my journey to becoming alive again.

Going to physical therapy was almost as regular as taking my vitamins. No less than three times a week I was attending sessions for one thing or another that was malfunctioning due to injury. As the years passed, I went less and less. But the equipment in my home kept increasing to help strengthen my muscles.

Once my muscles were strengthened then I had to get the memory of the injury removed from them. I went to *Intuitive Touch*, owned by my friend, Anita Norwood. She is a massage therapist. She worked with my body to retrain the muscles to relax and no longer constrict at the point of injury; that constriction was causing the pain. She told me that the memory of the violence had to be removed from the muscles. Once she removed the memory the pain in my legs disappeared.

Then, I learned that I needed more supplements in my diet. I must have taken almost everything that was available on the market. Mannetech, Herbalife, Noni Juice, Melaleuca Wellness Products, Juice Plus (freeze-dried fruit and vegetables in capsules), and Young Living Essential oils and natural products all played a part towards improving my health.

I had to regain health on three levels: spirit, soul and body. I went to see Dr. Z for the soul damage and I also attended a special class to bring balance to my mental health. Robin Rayford, my pastor's wife, taught a class, *Understanding Yourself.* By profession, she is a clinical psychologist. She knew how to use the Word of God to bring healing to a troubled mind. For nine months I attended that class. It brought about a birth of new hope.

My pastor and his wife work together as a dynamic duo for spiritual health and wellness. Pastor Stanley E. Rayford would pick up where Robin left off. I thought they compared notes before Sunday morning. I learned that neither conferred with the other. God so coordinated them on Sunday that later it surprised them to learn they were both teaching and preaching on the same subject.

Midweek, I went to Bible Class to stay encouraged until Sunday services. I tell you, it took all the energy I could muster to keep my own schedule. Somewhere between doctors' appointments, I found time to slip in a nap or two.

God used everything available to me as help for my journey back to wholeness. As I recovered more and more of what I lost, I wanted to help others. I wasn't strong enough to get a job, but I needed to use this whole experience to help others.

Somewhere, I birthed an idea to write a book. I looked at all those books I read. They served as my lifelines. Those writers went through tough experiences and took time to write them down. Surely, I learned something through all my trials that could help somebody else. Yes, I would write a book.

I didn't have a clue how to begin. I started with my journal notes. Filled with purpose, I typed them and thought, *now I'm ready to go.*

However, as I went over my notes, I found they were nothing but a mass of anger in print. How would I start writing?

I asked around and I learned about writer's conferences, where I listened to other writers, learned from instructors, and wrote something for others to critique. They helped me learn.

I attended a daylong conference at Oakland University and discovered that writers had to be readers first. I read about the fundamentals of writing—the basic tools—and practiced using them.

Then I found a writer's guild. It was intimidating at first. These people had it all together, so I kept my mouth shut, kept my pen taking notes, and kept learning. Someone recommended I subscribe to the *Writer's Digest Magazine* to receive monthly tips on what's hot in the business. Was there no end to this writing? The horizons kept expanding.

Then came the day when I had to give my writings to someone else to read, and wait for an evaluation. That was the scariest part of all. Writers' critique sessions sometimes hurt. Writers agree that those words on that page are their babies. Don't touch a one.

The groups of peers made corrections with their red pens and then returned their verdict. I sat there, dry-mouthed, ready to run, but to my amazement I received rave reviews.

Dear God, do You think I can do this?

Somehow it seemed He told me yes.

The hardest part of writing was accepting mentors. To help, they would have to get into my private space, and I wasn't sure I could tolerate that. Most of them didn't even ask permission.

It's amazing how, when once you start the journey, the teachers appear. An adage, "the teacher will teach when the student is ready" is true, and they were a great help. Next, I found that teachers not only gave to me but that I had something to deposit in their lives.

Support systems kept fanning the flame of my life by people who refused to let me abandon my purpose. When I was around such people, their enthusiasm lifted me out of the hole of helplessness.

They taught me to discover the hidden me. They also taught me how to dig deep and discover the unique skills buried under the rubble of my damaged emotions. While vocational rehabilitation is good for some folks, I couldn't rely on it to establish my new identity or give me a new passion for living. I realized that it was my life and I needed to find out what worked. If nothing changed, it's because I didn't try hard enough.

47

Conclusion

Romans 8:28: *And we know that all things work together for good to them that love God, to them who are the called according to his purpose.*

This scripture helped me to understand that nothing escaped the watchful eye of God. He took my worse circumstances and turned them around for my good.

During blissful times, I bragged about my strength in God, but didn't know how little I had. However, when misfortunes occurred, such as divorce, the death of a loved one, a child leaving home prematurely, or false accusations, these events challenged my faith. I discovered that I had to lean and depend on God. He worked out everything for my good. Truth prevailed.

From the age of 39 to 50, I had to face the truth and mature. The self-defeating habits had to go, even if I wasn't ready to make the necessary adjustments. God, strengthened me, took me through troubles; and I matured.

The psalmist stated in Psalms 119:71: *It is good for me that I have been afflicted, that I might learn thy statutes.*

I agree with the psalmist. Afflictions helped me to develop an intimacy with God. I learned what pleased Him and what didn't. I had to make some rather painful adjustments. Sometimes my troubles created a friction in my friendships. It allowed me to focus more on God's instructions and directions than man's. While I attended to my problems, it made me absent to my family and friends. These are some of the changes I made. I changed churches twice, abandoned a career, and made new alliances. All this was necessary for a new beginning.

God told me one day, *"Push until you see the change."*

I thought He was talking about the acronym P.U.S.H: *Pray until something happens.*

He said: *"Of course I want you to continue praying until something happens, you should never abandon prayer. But, I want you to push out all thoughts that keep you afraid. Push past those traditions of society that have you bound as a woman and an African-American. Push past those church traditions that tell you what to wear and where to go. Do not let anyone or anything keep you in a box of limitation. I want you to learn how-to please Me. So, I can teach you how to burst out of your cocoon of depression and fly—not like the butterfly—but like the eagle.*

When trouble tries to overcome you, I want you to fly above it. When the storms of suffering begin to blow, I want you to remember I have given you an opportunity to grow. See yourself already through it, because I will bring you through."

The transition from my old life to the new has been so painful that I wasn't sure I would survive, physically, mentally, or spiritually. Thank God, I made it.

For me, from ages twenty-two to thirty-nine, I lived in a marriage filled with infidelity and lies. I felt bound by the traditions of the church to keep trying. It wasn't working, yet I stayed. It was a relief when forced to face the truth. I stayed in denial as long as I did because I didn't want to go through the emotional pain. I retarded my personal growth.

Getting shot forced me to make the necessary changes. I could not run from my problems and hide behind the drama and thrill of my job. I had neither job nor a dysfunctional marriage to distract me. No one to blame for the pain and no institution to hide behind. I either fought against all obstacles in my way to bring about a change or remain miserable. I remember crying out to God, "I don't want to fight."

He said, *"Your children need to see you fight for what is right; especially your daughter."*

During my many challenges, I learned to fight and "how-to" make the necessary changes. I cried all the way to the attorney's office, and all through the preparations for trial. I cried while on the witness stand during trial, and I cried when I won. I didn't realize that all the battles were changing me into a stronger and more courageous person. I discovered, after the pain was gone, that I liked the new and improved me.

I learned that:

- What I do (vocation) is not who I am
- I can reinvent myself at anytime
- Leaning on God is important to overcoming troubles
- Recovery is hard work
- Restoration is worth the effort

My prayer is that anyone who is struggling on this road to recovery will read this book and find hope. Hope is God's merciful gift. Perhaps this book will inspire you to write *your* story. Yours is unique, you know. Tell it!

Afterword

Scriptures I found helpful for strength and encouragement:

- Ephesians 6:10: *Be strong in the Lord and in the power of his might*

- Philippians 4:13: *I can do all things through Christ which strengtheneth me.*

- Romans 8:28: *And we know that all things work together for good to them who love God and are the called according to His purpose.*

- Joshua 1:9: *Have I not commanded thee? Be strong and of a good courage; be not afraid, neither be thou dismayed, for I the Lord will go with thee whithersoever thou goest.*

- Romans 8:37: *Nay, in all these things we are more than conquerors through Him that loved us.*

- Matthew 19:26:...*But with God all things are possible.*

- Job 13:15: *Though he slay me yet will I trust in Him*

God not only talked to me directly, but He used many human beings to help me with my recovery, so keep your eye out to find people or places that will encourage you to excel. In Myles Munroe's book, *Maximize Your Potential,* he cautions us to be careful of the environment that we keep around us.

- Pinpoint your goal and decide what you need to achieve it.

- Seek out people and organizations that will support such a dream.

- But don't be a receiver only, you must help others to achieve their goals, too.

- Sometimes you are the mentor. Sometimes you need a mentor. Both positions are powerful.

- Pour what you know into someone else, and, as Myles Munroe says, "Die Empty".

The following is a list describing my support systems. Each helped to drag me out of the pit of despair:

Midwives for Jesus-Travailing Women: a group of women, who have been spiritually pregnant with ideas, visions and dreams by God. The women joined to gather in strength vowing to be a midwife to the dream. We left no one stunted in her growth if she would do the work to grow. We identified the enemies or obstacles to success and with the help of the Holy Spirit, the group travailed and achieved victory.

The Lydia Circle: Evangelist Minetta Hare founded this group. Her vision was to find a group of Christian businesswomen to meet early in the morning for breakfast, and have companionship before going to work. It was open to those, with or without a business, who loved God. It gave me a place to believe that one day all would be well. It gave me spiritual help, too. The spiritual power spilled over to a weekly prayer line. The telephone line of women prayed and saw miraculous results. I benefited from these anointed prayers.

Glory Girls' Reading Group: Denise Stinson founded this brainchild. She is a literary agent and the publisher of Walk Worthy Books. This group meets every two months reading Christian-based books. The books are fiction and non-fiction. I want my book chosen as a selected reading. This club gave to me when I needed it, and now I want my book to help someone else overcome his or her trouble.

American Christian Writers Association: Detroit, president, Pamela Perry. This group helped to stress the need for Christians to write. It is time for the voice of the Christian writer. I needed much help to encourage me to write and tell the goodness of the Lord.

The Called and Ready Writers: Minister Mary Edwards, founder. She wanted to help people get the shoebox of written materials from under the bed and into print. She found avenues to have our writings published. She stressed earning a living also. Mary gave us opportunities to write.

Detroit Writers' Guild: one of the oldest African-American writing guilds, where I learned the basics of writing. I think it was infectious being around all those writers. I had to write. I started, equipped with journals thinking the material found in them was a book. I learned the material was the seed to my future. It was this guild that stirred up my thirst to take it to another level and write a book.

Restoration Fellowship Tabernacle (RFT): Pastor Stanley and his lovely wife Robin Rayford are a dynamic duo for change. If you are willing to put in the effort to change, they will equip you with the tools to get there. They take it a step further by walking with you along the way, saying positive, affirming words that you can make it. This church is one of the best-kept secrets in the church community. If the routine of church attendance has you in a rut, then you need to visit RFT.

The class *Understanding Yourself,* taught by Robin Rayford, went back to the foundation of the formative years to the present. Childhood set the stage for who you are today. If you don't like what you see today, go back and see where you began the journey in life. We learned that obstacles in life may cause detours. Most folks detoured. Robin showed us how to make the necessary adjustments to get back on track.

Harvest Christian of Michigan and International: Pastor Norman Chaney and his lovely wife Barbra founded this church. I needed the love and acceptance I found there to heal my wounds.

Understanding How to Handle Issues Jesus' Style. taught by then Assistant Pastor Stanley Rayford and Robin, an unusual class to discover in a church setting. It dealt with all our issues.

Understanding God and His Covenants: this course, written by Patricia Beall Gruitts, was a good refresher course. It reminded me why Christ died and the agreement he made with me. I relearned the principles of the doctrine and asserted my covenant rights to be healthy again spirit, soul and body,

Greater Grace Temple (GGT), Detroit: the late Bishop David Ellis pastored this church. He was a friend to the end. He thought I was a special young woman with potential. He did not let my strange ways run him off. He worked at those unique ways by teaching me to stretch beyond my comfort zone. He was a cheerleader and friend. His death left a void. God gave me a host of others who picked up the baton. One of those was his son, Bishop Charles Ellis III, who is a chip off the old block with his own twist added in. Both were kind and instrumental in my recovery. GGT is a church that has over 250 ministries; it is a beacon light in the community.

Valorie Burton, Telecoach: Rich Minds, Rich Rewards gave free Internet life coaching and a free one-on-one coaching too. This woman helped to focus the theme and the purpose of my book. She gave back freely what she had received from God.

Dr. Jorge Zuniga, my psychiatrist and fellow patients were the lifelines for my mental health. Who would have believed that people who are labeled mentally ill would have answers and hopes among some dark times? There is a gold mine of intelligence, love, caring and hope among the mentally challenged.

Finally, remember who you are and learn how to transfer the skills that are buried under the rubble of damaged emotions. While vocational rehabilitation is good for some folks, don't rely on anybody to tell you who or what you do best. God alone knows that, and you need to ask Him. In the end, however, you are responsible to obey His leading. If nothing changes, it's because you didn't exert enough effort. God has provided, and it's up to us to take anything we need from His lavish storehouse.

Bibliography

1. *The Bible.* King James Version.

2. Burton, Valorie. *Rich Minds, Rich Rewards: 52 Ways to Enhance, Enrich, and Empower Your Life.* New York: Strivers Row, 2001.

3. Chesley, Roger. "Wounded Officer Leaves Hospital." *Detroit Free Press* 21 Dec. 1992 metro ed.

4. Foster, Cheryl. *Broken to be Made Whole.* Pennsylvania: Son Rise, 1992.

5. Gruits, Patricia. *Understanding God and His Covenants.* Michigan: Peter Pat, 1985.

6. Kaysen, Susanna. *Girl Interrupted.* New York: Vintage Books, 1993.

7. Malkamus, George. *Why Christians Get Sick.* North Carolina: Hallelujah Acres, 1995.

8. McCourt, Frank. *Angela's Ashes: A Memoir.* New York: Touchstone, 1996.

9. Munroe, Myles. *Maximizing Your Potential: Keys to Dying Empty.* Shippenburg: Destiny Image, 1996.

10. Nasar, Sylvia. *A Beautiful Mind: The Life of Mathematical Genuis and Nobel Laurate John Nash.* New York: Touchstone, 1998.

11. *The New International Webster Pocket Dictionary of the English Language.* Australia: Trident, 2001.

12. Traylor, Arnita. *"Transcript Docket No. 93-02443,"* *Recorder's Court.* Detroit: June, 1993.

About the Author

Denise A. Smith earned a Bachelors of Arts in Sociology from the University of Michigan. She worked, as a probation officer, for the State of Michigan, intermittently from 1974 to 1993. As a licensed minister, playwright, and freelance writer, Smith ministers to the downtrodden, depressed, and the hopeless.

Denise has been married to L.C. Smith, Jr. for seven years. They currently reside in Detroit, Michigan. They have a blended family of two daughters, Angela Thomason and Angela Clemmons, two sons, Aaron and Adam Thomason, and a wonderful son in law, Eric Clemmons. They are the proud grandparents of Nathan Dyer and Mali, Maya, and Moriah Clemmons.

0-595-30907-0